THE COUGAR

THE COUGAR

Beautiful, Wild and Dangerous

PAULA WILD

Douglas & McIntyre

Douglas and McIntyre (2013) Ltd.
PO Box 219
Madeira Park, BC, Canada VON 2HO
www.douglas-mcintyre.com

Cataloguing data available from Library and Archives Canada
ISBN 978-1-77162-002-4 (cloth)
ISBN 978-1-77162-003-1 (ebook)

Edited by Pamela Robertson
Cover and text design by Diane Robertson
Cover photograph by Thomas Kitchin and
   Victoria Hurst, All Canada Photos.
Additional photo credits: iStock photo—p. 117; Thinkstock—front
   cover top, text pp. 2–3, 6, 8–9, 10, 17, 20, 21, 33, 37, 72, 104, 125,
   127, 129, 141, 147, 168, 197, 244, 269, insert pp. 1, 2, 3, 4 bottom, 5,
   8, 9, 10 bottom right, 14 bottom, 15 top and middle, 16; Washington
   Department of Fish and Wildlife Karelian Bear Dog Program—p. 11;
   author photo—Rick James.
Maps by Roger Handling, Terra Firma Digital Arts
Indexed by Ellen Hawman
Printed and bound in Canada
Text printed on acid-free paper

We gratefully acknowledge the financial support of the Canada Council for the Arts, the British Columbia Arts Council, the Province of British Columbia through the Book Publishing Tax Credit and the Government of Canada through the Canada Book Fund for our publishing activities.

Note: This book contains information about cougar attacks. Like all wild animals, cougars are unpredictable. All recommendations regarding safety and defence are made without guarantee on the part of the author or Douglas and McIntyre (2013) Ltd. The author and publisher disclaim any liability in connection with the use of this information.

This book is dedicated to all the individuals and organizations who contribute to our knowledge of cougars and support the conservation of these magnificent creatures.

And to Dave Eyer, for his generous gifts of time, expertise, encouragement and friendship, and for teaching me how to be safe in the bush.

CONTENTS

Cougars are without doubt the epitome of the predator
species, fascinating creatures, the embodiment of the
spirit and aura of vast, rugged and uninhabited places.

—JUDD COONEY, "Big Cats Are Back"

The largest cat in Canada and the second largest in the US is known by many names but is most often called cougar, mountain lion or puma. As the widest ranging big predator in the western hemisphere, cougars roam from alpine to ocean and favour forested areas and rugged terrain that allows them to sneak up on their prey. Like other large predators, cougars play an important role in healthy ecosystems.

CHAPTER 1:
Paw Prints in the Snow

One of the most legendary and least understood
mammals of North America.

—DR. CATHY SHROPSHIRE, wildlife biologist,
Wildlife Mississippi Magazine

Heavily falling snow covered our footsteps almost as quickly as we made them. The fat white flakes, the forest around us and the arrival of twilight meant visibility was fading fast. And right in front of us, filling with snow as we watched, were the large paw prints of a cougar.

Our pickup was parked a couple of kilometres (about a mile) from the small logging and pulp mill community of Port Alice on northern Vancouver Island, British Columbia. We'd pulled off Highway 30 onto the SE Main, a logging road at the bottom of the hill heading out of town, to retrieve our thermos from the back of the truck. But now, following the tracks into the woods toward a small creek, our thoughts were on cougars. As the snow silently erased the paw prints I peered between the alders and up into their branches with equal measures of apprehension and excitement.

Elusive, graceful, powerful. Whether they've seen one in the wild or not, most people are fascinated by the big cat called cougar, puma, mountain lion and approximately forty other names. And the animal's size is part of the allure. Although it's not the norm, there are records of cougars measuring close to three metres (slightly over nine feet) long from the tip of the nose to the end of the tail. It's said that in 1936, John Huelsdonk, known as the Iron Man of the Hoh River on Washington's Olympic Peninsula, shot a cougar that stretched out to 3.35 metres (11 feet). Possibly the heaviest cougar on record was killed by an Arizona government worker in 1923. It weighed more than 125 kilograms (276 pounds). And that was after the intestines had been removed.

But don't let their size mislead you about the cat's speed and agility. Exceptionally long legs make cougars Olympic-class athletes when it comes to jumping. They've been observed leaping 5.5 metres (18 feet) straight up from a standstill, 18.5 metres (60 feet) down from a tree and nearly 14 metres (45 feet) horizontally onto the back of a deer. Noted conservationist, author and former cougar hunter Roderick Haig-Brown wrote that the big cat's "muscles are powerful enough to swing his weight completely around in mid-air." Cougars can run up to 72 kilometres (45 miles) per hour for a short distance, and even a smaller 45-kilogram (100-pound) cougar is capable of taking down a 318-kilogram (700-pound) elk.

Cougars are the fourth-largest cat on the planet and the biggest in Canada. The only feline of greater size in the Americas is the jaguar, which is primarily found south of the United States. Cougars were one of the most widely distributed large mammals in North and South America, but their populations were severely impacted by bounty hunting in the early to mid-twentieth century. In 2011 the United States declared the eastern cougar extinct and, aside from a small group of endangered Florida panthers, no one knows if any of the big cats are breeding east of the Mississippi River. But cougar numbers are stable and even increasing in many areas of western Canada and the United States, and some are even making their way to the Midwest and beyond.

At different times throughout the centuries humans have viewed cougars as mythical icons or mortal enemies, and called the big cats abject cowards or bloodthirsty killers. And cougars have the distinction of being classed as both predator and prey. During the bounty years, hunters were paid to shoot them; now most jurisdictions require people to pay for the privilege of doing so. Today, cougars are seen as symbols of agility, sex and power, and are frequently used as mascots for sports teams and in advertising campaigns. "Cougar" has also become the popular slang term used to describe mature women who prefer romantic liaisons with men a decade or more younger than themselves.

Although cougars normally claim the wild backcountry as home, it's not unusual for a big cat to casually stroll through a suburban subdivision under cover of darkness. Or to occasionally appear in such unlikely urban locations as the parking garage of the Fairmont Empress Hotel in British Columbia's capital city of Victoria. So, how does a cougar mysteriously materialize in a busy downtown area without being captured or shot somewhere along the way?

Part of the reason is their large padded paws, which allow the cats to travel in near silence. And they're masters at blending in, which is one reason they're sometimes called ghost cats. Even people who work in cougar country rarely see them in the wild. But that doesn't mean they aren't there. Odds are that one has watched you walk through the woods while you've been totally oblivious to its presence. And that's part of what makes the cougar an icon of all that is beautiful, wild and dangerous.

A cougar's muscular front legs make it the Popeye of the animal kingdom. These legs, combined with oversized paws and razor sharp claws, make the big cat a formidable hunter capable of taking down prey as large as a full grown elk. *Photo courtesy Cougar Mountain Zoo*

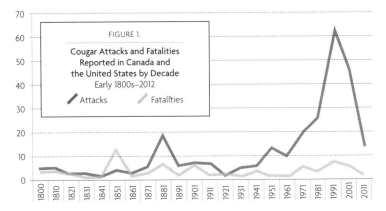

FIGURE 1.

Cougar Attacks and Fatalities
Reported in Canada and
the United States by Decade
Early 1800s–2012

Attacks   Fatalities

Although cougar attacks are extremely rare, they have increased significantly since the 1970s. Knowing the appropriate way to respond to a cougar can decrease the odds of an encounter becoming an attack and an attack resulting in a fatality. *Graph prepared by David G. Eyer*

In the last two hundred years there have been 252 documented attack incidents in Canada and the US, involving 255 cougars and 281 people. And statistics show that attacks on humans have increased significantly in recent years. In "Factors Governing Risk of Cougar Attacks on Humans," an article in the spring 2011 issue of *Human-Wildlife Interactions*, published by the Jack Berryman Institute of Utah State University, wildlife researchers David Mattson, Kenneth Logan and Linda Sweanor noted the number of "confirmed attacks resulting in human death and fatalities increased four to fivefold between the 1970s and 1990s."

In the overall scheme of things, however, cougar attacks are extremely rare. A person is far more likely to be killed in a car accident, by a domestic dog or even by a bee sting. Of course, the odds of seeing a big cat or having an encounter with one is higher for people who live, work or recreate in cougar territory. And as urban sprawl continues and more people venture into wilderness areas, encounters are becoming more common.

Most people don't think about cougars unless one is seen in the neighbourhood or an attack makes the news. After such incidents, while walking the dog in the woods or even relaxing in my rural backyard, I've wondered, "Could it happen here?" More frequently than I'm comfortable with, the answer is "Yes." I've also asked myself, "Was the attacked person doing anything I don't normally do?" The answer is often "No."

At times I've reassured myself by recalling an article I once read about a September 1916 attack near Cowichan Lake in the interior of southern Vancouver Island. One afternoon around 2:00 p.m., eleven-year-old Doreen Ashburnham and eight-year-old Tony Farrer were walking along a trail looking for a pony. They were less than a kilometre (about half a mile) from home when they spotted a cougar crouched on the path ahead. The children turned and ran. Ashburnham later told a reporter, "The cougar sprang from about 35 feet and landed on my back, throwing me forward onto my face. He chewed on my shoulder and bit chunks off my butt. Tony attacked him with the bridle he was carrying. They fought for 200 yards down the trail. The cougar scratched the skin off Tony's back turning his shoulders, hips and legs into ribbons of flesh and ripped the flesh off his scalp until it was hanging off the back of his head by six hairs."

Despite Ashburnham's injuries and Farrer yelling for her to save herself, the girl raced to her friend. "I jumped on the cougar's back and started hitting it on the head. I reached around and put my arm in his mouth so he'd stop biting Tony—you can see where I got nicely chewed up in a few thousand places—and I managed to scratch his eyes a little bit and it finally let go." Covered with blood, the children staggered home. "I remember my father taking Tony's clothes off and throwing them on the bathroom floor," Ashburnham said. "To this day I can see blood running out of the bathroom."

Long and exceptionally strong rear legs mean cougars are capable of leaping phenomenal distances: 5.5 metres (18 feet) straight up from a standstill, 18.5 metres (60 feet) down from a tree and nearly 14 metres (45 feet) horizontally onto the back of a deer.

Although they survived, both children were badly injured. Farrer required 175 stitches to his head alone and was hospitalized for a lengthy period. Ashburnham's right arm was badly mauled and she developed blood poisoning. A few days after the incident, an underweight two-and-a-half-year-old cougar with cataracts was found in the area and shot. In 1917, on behalf of the king of England, the Governor General of Canada presented the Albert Medal to Ashburnham—the youngest female recipient at the time—and Tony—the youngest recipient ever—for "gallantry in saving life on land."

The bravery of these two youngsters was impressive, and I thought if they could fend off a cougar, perhaps I could too.

Although eight-year-old Tony Farrer and eleven-year-old Doreen Ashburnham were severely injured, they fought off the cougar that attacked them. They were successful because they stuck together and focused their blows on the cougar's face and eyes. In 1917 they were awarded the Albert Medal for "gallantry in saving life on land." *Photo courtesy Kaatza Station Museum and Archives P985.4.1*

But the incident raised some questions. It's likely the cougar that attacked Ashburnham and Farrer did so because cataracts made it difficult for it to see and hunt. Out of 255 cougars involved in attack incidents over the past two hundred years, the condition of 168 is unknown. As for the others, 40 were classed as skinny or starving, 6 were injured or sick and 41 were healthy. And fifty-three percent of the victims were adults. So it isn't just sick, starving or injured cougars attacking children. Sometimes healthy, mature cougars—even ones that have recently eaten—stalk and attack adult humans. I wondered if it was simply a case of being in the wrong place at the wrong time. Or was something else going on? And what about the stories of particularly aggressive cougars on Vancouver Island and in southern California?

My great-grandfather, Frank Hicks, was buddies with Theodore Roosevelt, one of the most famous big game cougar hunters in North America, and I saw my first live cougar in Washington state before I could walk. Since then, I've found fresh tracks on northern Vancouver Island, seen what a guide referred to as "mountain lion poo-poo" in Mexico and heard a cougar scream in the green space behind my home. But until I began research for this book, I knew little about the big cats. I wasn't sure what to do if I saw a cougar, and didn't know the best way to prevent or survive an attack.

But my interest wasn't solely driven by fear. I also knew the cougar was a remarkable animal and that as a large predator, it played a significant role in nature. I wondered if cougar populations would continue to rebound or if, as some say, they're in danger. What would happen if cougars disappeared? As I studied the situation it became apparent that cougar populations and people's perceptions of the big cats are intimately connected, and that this relationship has the potential to profoundly affect the environment.

CHAPTER 2:
Lord of the Forest

The cougar has always been a power animal.

—MAX PETERSON

Old Man was mad at Mountain Lion. The short, chunky upstart had stolen his leftover grub while he was snoozing. It wasn't that Old Man was still hungry; it was the principle of the matter. He'd created Mountain Lion and it was time for the cat to show some respect. Dropping to his hands and knees so he could walk like a bear, Old Man followed Mountain Lion's tracks over humpbacked hills and through boggy swamps. Eventually he found a pile of freshly gnawed squirrel bones, the remains of his feast. Nearby, Mountain Lion slept on a sun-warmed rock, his belly round and full.

Slowly Old Man snuck up on the sleeping lion until he was close enough to grab its stump of a tail. Mountain Lion shrieked and begged for mercy. But after walking on all fours for a long time, Old Man was really angry. He grasped Mountain Lion's tail with both hands, put his feet behind the creature's head and pulled as hard as he could. The lion struggled and yowled but Old

Depending on its sex, the average weight of a full grown cougar is between 35 and 105 kilograms (77 to 230 pounds). The majority of the body is covered with short fur, usually in some variation of tan, grey or red, with creamy white on the underside and face. The cat's most distinctive feature is its thick, strong tail, which is approximately one-third the length of its body.

Man tugged until the cat's body was stretched out as far as possible. Then he placed his feet on Mountain Lion's rump and yanked on the tail until it was as almost as long as the body.

Satisfied that Mountain Lion would never steal his food again, Old Man dragged the feline all the way back to the fire where he'd cooked his squirrel meal. He stuck Mountain Lion's face and the tip of his tail into the smouldering embers until they were singed black. According to a Blackfoot legend, that's how mountain lions obtained sleek bodies, dark smudges on their muzzles and tails, and their most distinctive feature, a tail that's approximately one-third the length of their body.

People who see lynx, bobcats, golden labs and even large house cats from a distance often think they're cougars. It's estimated that seventy-five percent or more of reported cougar sightings are cases of mistaken identity. So if it doesn't have a long tail—about a metre (three feet) on an adult—it's not a cougar. As well as being a distinguishing appendage, the tail serves as a stabilizer, allowing a cougar to maintain its balance while chasing prey over rough terrain. And the combination of a long tail and a super-flexible spine means the cat can twist its body to change direction in mid-leap.

A cougar's tail is strong too. Biologist Penny Dewar discovered that when she and her husband, Percy, were studying cougars on Vancouver Island in the early 1970s. "After we treed a cougar Percy would shoot it with a tranquillizer dart," she explained. "We were maybe a little too conservative with the amount of drug we administered one as he staggered around like he was drunk while we tried to measure and examine him."

Dewar was 167 centimetres tall (five foot five) and only weighed 52 kilograms (115 pounds) at the time but that didn't stop the twenty-four-year-old from grabbing the cougar by the tail in an attempt to hold it still. "It was about two years old and probably weighed 100 pounds," she said. "We were about equal in size but not strength. Their tails are long and really thick, like a person's limb. With one flick of its tail, that cougar sent me flying into the trees."

Early Native populations living near the Great Lakes believed the twitching of a panther's tale was responsible for the storms and waves that tipped canoes and flooded villages. It's said Lake Erie was named after the tribe of the same name and that "Erie" is a short version of an Iroquois term meaning "long tail." And tribes on both sides of the Canada–US border feared the Underwater

Panther, a supernatural creature with the body of a panther, the horns of a deer and a ridge of upright scales along its back.

Scientists have documented the presence of big cats in the Americas since prehistoric times. Many people have heard about the sabre-toothed tiger, the giant jaguar and the massive American lion, weighing in at 500 kilograms (1,100 pounds). But little mention is made of their smaller cousin, the cougar. One theory suggests cougars evolved as a distinct species in North America around 400,000 years ago and gradually made their way to Central and South America. It's believed the North American cougar became extinct during the last ice age and the continent was later recolonized by a South American species.

Found only in the Americas, cougars originally roamed from northern Canada to the tip of South America and from coast to coast on both continents, including most adjacent islands. They have the greatest latitudinal distribution of any species of wild cat worldwide and are the widest ranging big predator in the western hemisphere. Cougars are highly adaptable and can live in almost any landscape. In coastal British Columbia they favour coniferous and deciduous forests, while Florida panthers prefer native upland forests and saw palmetto thickets. The mountainous desert areas of the southwestern United States and the tropical forests of South America are the prowling grounds of others. Cougars like canyons and escarpments and can survive in areas with little vegetation. But they're particularly fond of a mix of woods and open areas adjacent to streams, rivers and lakes.

The big cats can be found anywhere from sea level to rugged mountain slopes and often follow their prey up mountains in the summer and down into valley bottoms in the winter. They thrive in areas where there is a combination of adequate prey—primarily deer—and cover in which to stalk them. Ideal stalking habitat could include moderately dense shrubs, woodlands, tall grasses, trees or rough terrain—anything that allows a cougar to sneak up on its quarry.

One reason cougars do so well in such a wide range of habitat is that the colour of their coat tends to blend in no matter what the setting, which is a vital factor when stalking is the primary method of obtaining dinner. But perhaps the real secret of their adaptability lies in their willingness to eat any type of meat, from a mouse to a moose, including livestock and the occasional domestic pet.

The average adult male cougar weighs anywhere from 45 to 105 kilograms (100 to 230 pounds), with females being a bit smaller at 35 to 60 kilograms (77 to 130 pounds). When it comes to the heavyweights of the cat kingdom, only Siberian tigers, African lions and jaguars outrank cougars. Genetically, the cougar's closest relatives are the jaguar, the largest cat in the Americas, and the cheetah, which is primarily found in Africa and Asia. But there are striking differences between them. The cheetah is taller, lighter and faster than a cougar. It also has a weaker jaw and smaller teeth. In contrast, the jaguar is stockier and heavier and has the nastiest disposition of all three. Cougars and jaguars both have strong jaws and teeth capable of penetrating the skulls of large prey. Another distinguishing feature of jaguars is their husky cough-like roar. Solid hyoid bones in their throats make it impossible for cougars and cheetahs to create that sound.

What's the difference between cougars, mountain lions and pumas anyway? Absolutely nothing. *Guinness World Records* recognizes the big cat as having the most names of any animal. Like the majority of Canadians, I call them cougars. That word likely comes from Tupi, a Native Amazon language, and roughly translates as "false deer" or "predator the same colour as a deer." The term puma originated in the Quechua language of Peru, meaning "mighty magic animal." It's said early Incans were so enamoured of the cat they laid out their capital city, Cusco, in the shape of a puma. When explorers and Spanish conquerors arrived in the Americas they mistook cougars for female African lions. Natives told them the creatures lived in the mountains so the newcomers called them mountain lions. Other European explorers thought they were seeing tigers or panthers (a name sometimes used for leopards) so those names were also used.

Today, location is the primary influence on what the feline is called. In Canada the common name is cougar, while mountain lion is often used in the western United States. Catamount ("cat of the mountains") is still heard occasionally in New England, and in Florida the cat's known as a panther. Panther was widely used throughout Canada and the US until the mid-twentieth century but is now mostly heard east of the Mississippi River, particularly in the south. Puma is the term of choice in scientific circles and in South America. Cougar, mountain lion and puma are the most frequently used names in the United States and Canada.

The big cat has even had more than one scientific name. It was originally classified in the genus *Felis*, along with the lynx, the domestic cat and numerous other species. But when scientific evidence revealed cougars were more closely related to cheetahs and jaguars than small cats, the Latin name changed from *Felis concolor* to *Puma concolor*, giving the cat status as a unique New World species. Genetic analysis also suggests the number of subspecies is six rather than the former thirty-two. That would give North America one subspecies, *Puma concolor cougar*. As well as living in a wider variety of habitat, pumas in South America have a wider genetic variation, so they've been divided into five subspecies.

The *concolor* part of the big cat's name, meaning "one colour," has remained the same. Adult cougars are indeed mostly one colour, which can range from shades of tan to silver, slate grey and even red. Some have a ridge of darker hair running along the spine from head to tail. The fur on the belly, chest, throat and muzzle is creamy white, and there are distinct black markings on the muzzle and the tips of the tail and short, round ears. Long, delicate-looking whiskers sprout from the area between the cougar's mouth and nose, while more long white hairs accent the cat's vertical eyebrows. While there is no scientific documentation in the way of photographs or deceased animals, there are reports of black or chocolate-coloured cougars in many regions of North

A cougar's facial markings can be exquisitely beautiful. The grey, brown or reddish fur is accented by a white patch around the mouth and long, delicate white whiskers below the nose and along the vertical eyebrows. But what is most striking are the dark markings on the muzzle and around the eyes. *Photo by Robyn Barfoot*

and South America. And the Huron and Seneca cultures have stories referring to a White Lion, or White Panther Man.

Due to its prowess and mystique, the cougar is often heralded by indigenous people as a symbol of physical and spiritual strength. Both feared and revered, the animals were killed by Native peoples in ancient times not only to protect themselves from injury but as a means of gaining prestige and power. Although the meat was rarely eaten, cougar teeth, paws, claws, hides and sometimes heads were worn as signs of authority and rank, used as ceremonial regalia and employed by shamans to guard against enemies, illness and other misfortunes.

In Peru the Incas organized game drives by forming human circles and gradually driving pumas and other predators to the middle, where they were killed. Under cover of darkness Central American Natives lured puma to their death by imitating the calls of distressed prey on instruments made from hollowed-out animal bones and branches. But whether the big cats were killed by bolas, clubs or bows and arrows, there was usually some ceremonial ritual involved and the person slaying the animal often believed some of the cat's energy and skill would pass on to them.

Early in the last century, Aymara warriors in the Andes drank puma blood for courage, while the Cochiti Warriors Society in New Mexico only admitted men who had killed mountain lions and bears or who had slain and presented the scalp of an enemy Navajo. The Cherokees believed that by remaining awake throughout the seven days and nights of Creation, the cougar and owl achieved the highest level of purity and sacredness. As a reward for their faithful vigilance, the animals were given excellent night vision. The Cherokees honoured the big cat by calling it *Klandagi*, or Lord of the Forest. The Cheyennes considered the mountain lion a friend and provider, while the Apaches believed that hearing one scream foretold an imminent death. Panther clans were common among eastern tribes such as the Seminoles and Shawnees. And in the dense green rain forests of the Pacific Northwest, Washington state Natives told stories about mountain lions carrying fire from the Olympic Mountains to Mount Rainier each fall, accidentally starting forest fires along the way.

Even today, there are numerous cougar, panther and mountain lion clans throughout the Americas, although some are not as active as they were in the past. The mountain lion is prominent in the culture of the Pueblo peoples of the American southwest, where it is variously considered to be a supernatural patron of warriors and hunters, a protector and the most important of the Pueblo Beast Gods. One of the most amazing tributes to the big cat, the Shrine of the Stone Lions, can be found in Bandelier National Monument Park, 71 kilometres (44 miles) from Santa Fe, New Mexico. Crouching side by side with their tails extended behind them, the bodies of the weather-worn beasts are approximately 1.8 metres (6 feet) long and 0.6 metres (2 feet) high. They are surrounded by a rough rock wall open on the eastern side. Of special significance to both the Cochiti and the Zuni, it's believed these rare, life-size sculptures were carved by former residents of a nearby pueblo ruin, Yapashi, which may have been occupied between the thirteenth and sixteenth centuries. A similar shrine lies about 1.6 kilometres (a mile) away but one of the lions was dynamited by a scavenger around 1875.

Using plant-based dyes and small rocks, Natives painstakingly painted and pecked mountain lion images onto cliffs and rock faces and in caves throughout the southwestern United States. By chipping away at the dark varnish coating desert rocks, artists revealed the lighter-coloured rock beneath, bringing their visions to life. One of the most outstanding examples was found in

Often called the icon of Arizona's Petrified Forest National Park, this mountain lion petroglyph was discovered near Blue Mesa in 1934. The 38 by 15 centimetre (15 by 6 inch) rock carving was probably created in the twelfth or thirteenth century. It's notable for the shape of the mouth, possibly representing the flehmen response, which occurs when some animals open and curl their lips back when responding to certain smells such as urine or sex pheromones. *Photo by Katherine Hall*

1934 near Blue Mesa in what is now Arizona's Petrified Forest National Park. With its stylized feet and claws, long lean body and tail curving up over the spine, this mountain lion petroglyph is a classic example of early Native southwestern culture.

For many southwestern tribes the mountain lion is an icon of power, protection and friendship. It's revered by the Hopi as a guardian *kachina* (ancestral spirit) and associated with the colour yellow. In ancient times the Zuni believed mountain lions had the ability to facilitate communication between humans and spiritual deities. In some pueblos medicine men wore strips of mountain lion hide and claws around their necks and forearms as a safeguard against witches. Others called upon the predator's energy to both kill and cure.

Fetishes have long been part of Native American culture in the southwestern US. These small stone carvings are said to contain the spirits of the animals they resemble. In the past they were often used as talismans to guide individuals on journeys or to ensure good hunting by transforming from stone into living creatures that could chase down prey. As the big cat was a dominant prey god, mountain lion fetishes were highly valued, especially by hunters, warriors and shamans. Traditional renditions always depict the tail curving up over the spine while modern versions may show the tail hanging toward the ground or over the back and down the side. Modern characteristics associated with cougar fetishes include authority, leadership and self-confidence.

South of the US, the jaguar trumps the puma when it comes to physical presence and symbolism. Archaeological findings reveal jaguars on jewelry, pottery and carvings much more often than pumas. And while both cats are linked to the supernatural, jaguars are more closely identified with fertility and sexuality. Still, puma skins, claws and teeth were often used by Native groups as hunting trophies and indications of a noble presence and influence.

Although the felines often share the same habitat, they're not buddies. As James H. Gunnerson noted in *Icons of Power: Feline Symbolism in the Americas,* pumas and jaguars do fight each other and the pumas often win.

Considering how plentiful cougars are in western Canada today, it's surprising that they are so rarely featured in traditional Northwest Coast culture. When asked why, Andy Everson, a First Nations artist and member of the K'ómoks Band on the central east coast of Vancouver Island, said, "The cougar is not considered an ancestor so there is no crest figure representing it."

In comparison to other animals, cougar images are strangely absent from ancient First Nations cultural objects in British Columbia. Most representations, such as this totem pole that was carved at the village of Kitwanga in the Gitxsan territory around 1865, are found in the northern part of the province. *Photo by George Thorton Emmons (1910), courtesy University of Washington Libraries, Special Collections, NA3436*

A totem pole that does feature a cougar was carved in 1865 at the village of Kitwanga in the Gitxsan territory of northwestern BC. Natives told researcher Norman Tait that a cougar appeared by the upper Skeena River one day and killed a chief's daughter. Some of her relatives chased the cat into the water, destroyed it and adopted the animal as a family crest.

Lyn Hancock noted in her 1980 Simon Fraser University thesis that Stoney and Sarcee Natives in Alberta were terrified of cougars due to their aggressive and stealthy ways. She also mentioned that the Coast Salish of British Columbia only occasionally roasted, steamed or boiled cougar meat to eat. And that makes sense as coastal Natives could more easily access the abundant larder of the sea than creatures living in the thick forests where hunting was sometimes difficult. Cougar skins were considered valuable, however, and were worn as symbols of power and self-assurance. A ceremonial dance and story from the Nuu-chah-nulth on the west coast of Vancouver Island tells of a young boy slaying a ferocious cougar and throwing it on a fire. As the ashes of the dead cat drifted up from the flames they were transformed into mosquitoes, which like the cougar feast on the blood of their prey.

In the sixteenth and seventeenth centuries the Hurons and Senecas of southeastern Canada and the northeastern United States considered the panther a personal guardian spirit and carved elaborate pipes representing them. Some featured the long bodies and tails of the cats; others depicted panther men with brass or copper eyes. These power panthers were also used as embellishments on hair combs and war clubs.

Today, whether it's an object of worship or worry, the cougar remains culturally significant for many North and South American indigenous peoples. Ceremonies continue to be held at the Shrine of the Stone Lions and other sacred locations and many traditional beliefs are maintained. But it's unlikely that even the greatest of the old shamans could have foreseen the amount of attention that would be focused on the cougar in the future, the misconceptions that would surround the animal and the changes that would threaten its survival.

CHAPTER 3:
Mythical Icon
to Mortal Enemy

The most elusive...and shyest thing in the woods.

—ERNEST THOMPSON SETON,
Wild Animals at Home

The arrival of European settlers heralded a dramatic change in attitude toward cougars. While Natives revered and feared the big cats, newcomers to the land were divided in their views. Some saw the animals as cunning murderers and dastardly varmints best shot on sight; others considered them great hunters of their natural prey but cowardly when it came to confrontations with humans.

While travelling in North America during the late 1850s, Sir James Carnegie, the Ninth Earl of Southesk, made an observation about the stealth of the cougar that revealed sentiments common to the day: "Making out a small party of hunters or travelers, it will follow them for days, and watch their camp at night, till at last it discovers one of their number resting a little separate from his companions. Then, when all is dark and silent, the insidious puma glides in and the sleeper knows but a short awakening before its fangs are buried in his throat." Grief-stricken by the loss of his wife, the thirty-two-year-old had left Scotland to "travel in some part of the world where good sport could be met with among the larger animals" and in hopes of restoring his health. North American holidays that combined wilderness adventure and possibly restorative health benefits became popular with the British and North American upper class during the nineteenth century. For those who could afford it, these trips were a way to escape the tedium and trials of everyday life, prove one's manhood by experiencing potentially dangerous situations and collect entertaining stories to tell at dinner parties for years to come.

Carnegie's concerns about cougars were justified, as they do stalk their prey for long distances, sometimes for hours or even the better part of a day. And there are documented cases of the cats attacking people while sleeping and attempting to break into tents. But not everyone shared his unease. In *Wild Animals at Home*, Ernest Thompson Seton referred to the mountain lion as "the most elusive, sneaking, adroit hider and shyest thing in the woods." The wildlife artist, naturalist and author was a founding member of the Boy Scouts of America and was appointed Official Naturalist to the Government of Manitoba in 1892. A tall, rangy fellow with bushy hair and a signature mustache, Seton often disappeared into the backcountry for weeks at a time. He once noted that in twenty-five years of camping he'd never seen a cougar in the wild but was certain many had seen him.

In the chapter entitled "Sneak-cats Big and Small" he recalled a September 1899 trip with his wife in the High Sierras of California. Since the weather was fine they arranged their bedding on the ground. The next morning the horses were gone and the tracks of a large cougar were everywhere. "He had prowled into camp coming up to where we slept, sneaked around and smelt us over and—I think—walked down the alley between our beds," wrote Seton. "The horses were in danger but I think we were not."

As a naturalist, Ernest Thompson Seton enjoyed spending time outdoors conducting research for his wildlife paintings and books. He drew this sketch after an 1899 camping trip with his wife in the High Sierras of California. The couple never heard a sound but woke up one morning to find their horses gone and the paw prints of a mountain lion circling their bedding. *Sketch by Ernest Thompson Seton in* Wild Animals at Home, *1913*

Former US president and avid big game hunter Theodore Roosevelt shared Seton's lack of concern, and considered cougars the most cowardly of the big cats around humans. In 1916 he observed that although large male cougars often killed prey that an African leopard would hesitate to tackle, they rarely threatened people. "There is no more need of being frightened when sleeping in, or wandering after nightfall through, a forest infested by cougars than if they were so many tom-cats," he wrote in *A Book-Lover's Holidays in the Open.* "It is absolutely safe to walk up to within ten yards of a cougar at bay, whether wounded or unwounded, and to shoot it at leisure."

Whether cougars were considered killers or cowards was a matter of perception. While various nature lovers and big game hunters felt there was nothing to fear, many explorers and immigrants assumed cougars were related to the lions, tigers and leopards found in Africa and Asia. At different times each of those animals has borne the name "man-eater." So why wouldn't the big cats of the New World possess the same appetites and inclinations?

One of the earliest recorded instances of a cougar attacking a human took place in 1751. Philip Tanner was killed at the edge of the woods at Betty's Patch—now known as Lewisville—in Chester County, Pennsylvania. The fifty-eight-year-old owned a mill and lived nearby. It's believed he was scouting the area for timber to harvest when he died. A crouching cougar is chiselled on his tombstone.

In *Two Admirals: Sir Fairfax Moresby & John Moresby, A Record of a Hundred Years*, John Moresby recounted an 1853 incident at Fort Rupert on northern Vancouver Island. "Bear, deer and puma abound, the latter much dreaded and with reason," wrote the British naval officer, who was serving on the HMS *Thetis* at the time. "During our stay, whilst the women were gathering roots in the forest, one puma killed twelve girls, tearing them down one after another like a dog worrying sheep. We would gladly have avenged them, and the Indians were willing guides, but we had no luck in the impenetrable woods."

Events like these provoked fear and anger, prompting people to shoot cougars anytime they saw one. But there was another problem: many immigrants had no desire to live in the wilderness; they wanted to shape it to their wants and needs. So they sculpted the landscape into farms, ranches and communities, clearing

Many New World settlers considered cougars bloodthirsty killers that posed a serious threat to livestock and human life, so shot them on sight.

ground, planting crops, raising livestock and building towns as fast and as soon as they could. The prevailing attitude of the day was that the land, and all that was in and on it, was theirs to exploit as they saw fit. Trees were for firewood, fences and buildings while fertile soil was for planting vegetables, fruit trees and grains, and for raising chickens, cattle and sheep. Deer, buffalo, grouse and other indigenous wildlife were there to stock the pantry.

Large predators, such as wolves, bears and pumas, were another matter. They were also eaten but not as often. Wolf meat tended to be stringy and tough and was often regarded as unsuitable for consumption unless a person was starving. According to an 1868 article in *The Saint Pauls Magazine*, edited by Anthony Trollope, "The flesh of the wolf may be taken to be about the rankest of carrion in creation, not even excepting the common vulture and turkey buzzard."

Of the three, bear meat was, and still is, the most commonly consumed. Sweet and on the greasy side, it's said to taste similar to pork. Two-year-old cubs were considered prime, especially if killed in the spring while they were still eating roots and berries and before they had an opportunity to feast on rotting, spawning salmon. As for cougar meat, it wasn't eaten on a regular basis but those who tried it generally liked it, with some even considering it a delicacy. Those who have tried cougar meat say it resembles veal or lamb in flavour, taste and texture but can be dry as the fat content is low. Charles Darwin, who ate cougar while exploring South America, noted, "The flesh is very white and remarkably like veal."

Even today, cougar meat is deemed a tasty addition to a cook's repertoire by some. While living in Hagensborg, a small community in the Bella Coola Valley on the central coast of BC, Kristeva Dowling learned that although cougar lard is rare, it makes excellent pastry. "The very best way to cook cougar, however," she said, "is to stir-fry it with snow peas and water chestnuts. Or make a real smoked ham with the hind end."

Early settlers, like modern day ranchers, were more concerned with cougars preying on livestock than as potential entrees for the dinner table. And as settlement spread, conflicts were inevitable. By the mid-1800s large tracts of old-growth forest—some say more than fifty percent of what existed in the eastern United States—had been transformed into agricultural land. The same changes were taking place in Canada, just at a slower, less dramatic pace. The loss of habitat, accompanied by unrestricted hunting, resulted in a dramatic decrease in the deer population, and deer are a staple of many cougars' diets. So when deer were replaced with cattle, sheep, pigs, horses and domestic pets, the ever-adaptable cougar began hunting a different kind of prey.

South of the US the story was much the same. In northern Mexico, Jesuit missionary Joseph Oct wrote of flocks of thousands of sheep and goats in his mid-1700s diary, but noted, "The numbers of these animals would be even more remarkable were not about half of them devoured by tigers or leopards." Depredation of livestock by pumas became a serious problem in the Patagonia region of Argentina when newcomers created large sheep ranches and also heavily hunted guanacos, the llama-like animals that were the major prey for pumas in the area. Early records of this region also document many attacks by the big cats on horses and humans.

Depending on the season and various conditions, such as if a female is pregnant, nursing or feeding young, a cougar typically kills and eats the equivalent of one deer every seven to ten days. On occasion, however, a cougar has killed as many as fifty sheep and only fed off two or three. Perhaps domestic animals aren't as quick to vacate the scene of a slaughter as wild beasts, or if they're penned up are unable to do so, thus creating a slaying opportunity too good for a cougar to pass up. Or as Harley Shaw speculated in *Soul Among Lions*, the panicked behaviour of livestock may put a cougar's chase and kill instinct into overdrive. Whatever the case, it's easy to see how the cats became known as "bloodthirsty beasts" and "ravenous brutes."

For early settlers it was a struggle to tame and control the land in order to survive. When problems arose, they usually had to deal with situations on their own. Since cougars attacked livestock, pets and sometimes people, they were seen as a threat to both livelihood and life. Nearly all settlers possessed firearms and most didn't hesitate to use them. And on occasion they employed more organized efforts to destroy predators. In *The Panther and the Wolf,*

Colonel Henry W. Shoemaker described a 1760 game drive led by Black Jack Swartz in Snyder County, Pennsylvania. Two hundred men accompanied by barking dogs formed a circle roughly 48 kilometres (30 miles) in diameter and then closed in while shouting, shooting guns and blowing whistles. On that particular day they killed 41 cougars, 109 wolves, 112 foxes, 114 mountain cats (lynx and bobcats), 17 black bears, 12 wolverines, 3 fishers, an otter and a grizzly bear.

As the natural habitat disappeared, so did the wildlife. The animals that remained were ruthlessly slain—some for food, others for sport. The population of white-tailed deer dropped so dramatically that they were classed as uncommon in Connecticut by 1700. And as their primary prey vanished, the number of cougars dwindled. By the mid- to late 1800s it was believed that all cougars in the US had been exterminated east of the Mississippi River except for a small population in Florida. In Canada, it was estimated that there were as few as forty cougars left in Ontario by the 1800s.

As people moved west, they faced the same conflicts with predators. Even in the early days of settlement, Vancouver Island had a reputation for a high density of cougars. And they seemed particularly fond of settlers' livestock. Eric Duncan moved from the Shetland Islands to central Vancouver Island in 1877. In his memoir *Fifty-Seven Years in the Comox Valley*, he wrote: "One day my aunt (a tiny woman), hoeing potatoes in a field, was puzzled by the persistent squealing of a small pig in the bush alongside. Climbing the fence, she went towards the sound, and saw a cougar sitting on his haunches, holding up the pig in his mouth like a squirrel with a fir cone. She advanced, waving her hoe and calling out, as she would have done to a fence-breaking cow, and the surprised brute dropped his prey and slunk off. The pig, though badly mauled, survived."

Of course, those with larger herds of livestock couldn't be on constant guard with a stout stick and sharp tone of voice. Instead, they formed range and livestock associations and lobbied governments to initiate predator control programs. Folks back east had resolved their predator problem and people in the west were determined to do the same. And so the biggest cat in Canada and the US went from being a feared but always respected and often worshipped symbol of authority and power to a nasty piece of work to be exterminated at any cost.

CHAPTER 4:
From Predator to Prey

Anyone can kill a deer. It takes a real man
to kill a varmint.

—BEN LILLY, *The Ben Lilly Legend*

For most cougar hunters, the challenge of outsmarting a large predator and the thrill of the chase were far more rewarding than the payment earned. Near the end of his 1948 book *Hunting American Lions*, Frank C. Hibben described the cougar as a "fascinating, terrifying, and sometimes loveable cat." He should know: in the mid-1930s he spent a couple of years chasing them through the rugged canyon country of New Mexico conducting research for the Southwestern Conservation League. Hibben wrote about his experiences in a vivid style that made the reader feel as if they were part of the hunt, sharing the excitement and chaos right alongside him.

We had scarcely reached the edge of the cliff when we saw the lion. Old Crook was in the face of the beast and both of them were on a narrow jutting ledge that reached out over the depths of the Gila Canyon with a sheer drop of a thousand feet below them. First one and then another of the other hounds reached the little rocky point where the cougar had come to bay. The pinnacles and rough-edged cliffs echoed a roar of sound which united in a crescendo of furious howls, barks and yelps that would have done credit to a volcanic eruption of major proportions.

I think Homer and I too were yelling as we scrambled down over the rocks and ledges with our chaps flying and loose rocks and fragments rolling from beneath our feet. But any sound of exhilaration which we might have made was completely lost in the roar of the dogs as they faced the snarling lion. . .

So furious was the onslaught of noise and confusion that the cat had backed to the narrow edge of the cliff so that his tail and hind quarters hung over the shadows of the empty gorge below. A wisp of blood-flecked foam dripped from those cat jaws and whipped away in the wind. The ears of the beast were laid back flat against his head and the lips of his muzzle were curled up straight to reveal every white, gleaming fang down to its yellow base.

As the dogs crowded one another close, the lion unsheathed its claws and struck with a sidewise motion so quick that the movement was blurred to the human eye. Those raking, curved claws barely missed a dog with each strike, but still they crowded closer. The hounds behind pushed the ones in front into the very jaws of destruction. The long sweeping curve of those needle-sharp claws, or the bite of those white canines, would find a mark in a matter of seconds. The dog or the lion or both could make a miss-step of only inches to plunge themselves into destruction on the rough lava rocks in the canyon below us.

. . . The dogs had pushed old Bugger almost between the front paws of the lion. The cougar struck again and again with lightening rapidity. I could see the fleck of red flesh that showed where Bugger's shoulder had been torn by a claw. The dog caught himself with difficulty. . . and hung for a brief second on the very edge of the cliff scrambling for life.

. . . The great cat with the purchase of his hind paws barely on the edge of the rock cliff, leaped clear over the dog pack crowded in front of him. With two tremendous bounds he cleared the edge of the cliff and was running along a ledge just below us. The cat-like certainty and precision of that fleeing beast was amazing. A miscalculation of inches in any one of his great bounds would have meant certain death. The lion was running along the face of the cliff as though he had suction cups on those big round paws.

Although many cougar hunters experienced what Hibben called "a fever in the blood" when tracking a big cat, most weren't chasing cougars for scientific purposes. As settlers increased the pressure to rid the country of large predators, the extermination of the "noxious beasts" began in earnest. A timeline on The Cougar Fund's website states that, as early as 1684, Connecticut introduced a bounty on cougars. Over time, other states and provinces followed. Bounty hunters, and later government predator control agents, employed a variety of methods to kill the big cats, such as poison, trapping and tracking. But it wasn't easy. Cougars prefer fresh meat so poisoned bait didn't work on them nearly as well as it did on wolves. And pit and leg-hold traps, sometimes smeared with catnip and petroleum oil, weren't very effective either. Eventually everyone agreed: the best way to catch a cat was to chase it with hounds, tree it, then shoot it.

Initially, many bounty hunters were farmers and ranchers looking for opportunities to supplement their income. But when they realized decent money could be made, more than a few took up the occupation full time. Some viewed it as a vocation; others only responded to requests for assistance after a cougar had killed livestock. Eventually, the role of a bounty hunter evolved into a combination of community service worker and paid assassin. Although such large-scale killing would not be sanctioned today, in their era, bounty hunters were highly respected and many became folk heroes and legends in their own time.

One of the most renowned was Ben Lilly, a mystical mountain man who believed he could communicate with animals and see inside their bodies to understand them on a physical and emotional level. Born in Mississippi in 1853, Lilly became obsessed with big game hunting after singlehandedly killing a bear with a knife. His chosen career took him from to Arizona to Idaho and down to Mexico. After a trip with Lilly as a hunting guide, Theodore Roosevelt noted that although Lilly was not a large man, his "frame of steel and whipcord" was capable of walking

Ben Lilly was a small wiry man whose personal goal was to obliterate mountain lions and bears, which he called the "Cains of the world." Lilly lived outside most of his life and was known as a religious fanatic and mystic. He was fearless too; on occasion he engaged in paw-to-hand combat with only a knife as a weapon. *Photo, negative 6872, courtesy Palace of the Governors Photo Archives (NMHM/DCA)*

long distances without food, water or rain gear and never seemed to tire or mind rough terrain.

Frank Hibben took a three-day hike with Lilly in 1934. The eighty-year-old bounty hunter informed Hibben that bears and panthers were the "Cains" of the animal world and needed to be destroyed. Hibben had heard that Lilly was old and sick but what he found was a highly skilled woodsman who easily made his way across the landscape and who seemed to pick up panther sign by intuition and scenting the air like a dog. One evening Lilly led Hibben to a fresh panther kill and carved off a slab of venison for their dinner.

Lilly married twice and had several children who he supported but rarely saw. Preferring to be outside, the panther hunter disappeared for years at a time and pitied people who lived in towns and were forced to breathe "rancid" air. Lilly never indulged in alcohol, tobacco or coffee but regularly ate panther meat as he believed it increased his hunting abilities. Sundays were reserved for reading the Bible—if his dogs treed a panther on the Sabbath, he expected them to keep it there until Monday morning. Lilly shot most bears and panthers with a Winchester rifle but was also known to engage in paw-to-hand combat. His favourite weapon for this situation was a custom-made version of the bowie knife. He made his own knives out of scavenged steel, tempering them in panther oil.

As Lilly's legendary status grew so did the number of animals he was said to have killed. Estimates put the figure for cougars at somewhere between six hundred and a thousand. He sent panther, bear, Mexican grey wolf and other specimens to the Smithsonian in Washington, DC, and in later years informed people he was writing a book. It had two chapters: "What I Know About Bears" and "What I Know About Panthers." Lilly died in 1936 near Silver City, New Mexico.

Although Lilly wasn't overly fond of people, he loved and took good care of his hounds, which accompanied him everywhere. For cougar hunters, well-trained hounds provide keen noses for tracking, company when out on the trail and sometimes protection. In *The Intelligence of Dogs*, Stanley Coren noted that humans have used dogs for hunting since paleolithic times, and that some dogs, like Afghans, find their prey by sight while others, such as beagles, hunt by scent. The latter have wide nostrils angled toward the ground, making it easy for them to inhale the aroma of their prey's paw prints. They also pick up scent from tall grasses or bushes the animal has rubbed against. "A good dog will track beneath leaves and even snow," said long-time hunter George Pedneault, who started hunting cougars when he was thirteen. "I've seen them bury their heads in two feet of snow to get the scent."

Not all noses are created equal, however. According to Coren, humans have 5 million scent glands in their nostrils, beagles have 225 million and bloodhounds possess an astounding 300 million. But the nose is a funny thing; after being aware of a smell for a short time, it cuts out. Hunting hounds get around that by lifting their heads every few minutes to inhale some fresh air. While some are taking a short olfactory break, others are putting their noses back to the ground to search for the scent and once they've found it, begin baying again. That's why hounds work best in packs.

The type of bark, as well as its intensity and frequency, tells the hunter his dogs have found a scent and allows him to follow them. It also lets him know when the hounds are closing in on their quarry and when they've treed it. "A trained dog barks a certain way when they're on a cold trail, then lets out a long drawn out bawl [bark] as the trail warms up," explained Pedneault. "When they tree a cougar the barking becomes shorter and faster. Even from a distance you can tell what's happening by the type of bark."

Pedneault should know. Throughout his sixty-year career, he figures he's tracked more than three hundred cougars as a bounty hunter, on-call predator control agent for the government and guide on Vancouver Island.

"Cougars can go forever at a slow lope so if you pick up a travelling track you could be gone two or three days," he added. "But if you bust them and make them run, they're only good for about a thousand-foot sprint before being completely winded. They're only good for that short little burst and then they tree. A startled or full-bellied cougar will tree even faster."

Although a cougar could easily turn and kill a dog, many don't. The biggest danger occurs when a cat is defending cubs, which it will do no matter how large they are, or if it's cornered or shot and comes out of a tree injured instead of dead. That's why hunters tie up their dogs before taking aim with their rifles. Cougars can give hounds the slip by travelling over rough ground, doubling back or leaping up cliffs or down canyons where it's impossible for its human and canine pursuers to follow. Hunts can go on for hours or even days, resulting in exhausted dogs with hoarse-sounding barks and sore paws and noses. If a hunter is far from camp and forced to spend the night outside with few supplies, that's when Keeno, Old Red, Bugger or Buck might do double duty as "hot water bottles of the hunt." As Hibben wrote in *Hunting American Lions*, "Two or three hounds arranged around one's person will create a very satisfactory delusion of warmth, at least in those particular places."

Hounds often pick up a scent and follow it the wrong way. And it isn't always easy to turn them around. James T. Owen, commonly known as "Uncle Jimmy," threw pebbles at his dogs to get their attention. In 1906, he became the first game warden of the Grand Canyon Game Preserve, and on one hunt told

Theodore Roosevelt, "They think they know best and needn't obey me unless I have a nose-bag full of rocks."

Before radio telemetry collars, hounds often ran beyond the hearing and yelling range of their masters and could be gone for days and, on occasion, weeks. Jay C. Bruce, California's first state lion hunter, solved this dilemma by calling his hounds with a horn. Born in 1881, Bruce grew up near Wawona, in the western Sierra Nevada Mountains in what is now Yosemite National Park. He was enrolled at Heald's School of Mines and Engineering in San Francisco when the big earthquake of 1906 occurred and the resulting fire destroyed the building. Bruce returned to the rural life he loved and, along with a partner, built a sawmill. But after a work accident damaged his left hand, he lost both the mill and his house.

Incredibly strong and tenacious, Jay Bruce was the state of California's first mountain lion hunter. Two accidents meant he spent twenty years chasing lions with only one good eye and one good hand. The hand injury forced him to use a handgun instead of a rifle. He had to get close to the big cats, adjust his depth perception to compensate for his bad eye and have a very steady hand when it came time to shoot. *Photo courtesy Bruce family collection*

Limited by the type of work he could do and desperate to support his wife and four children, Bruce started hunting mountain lions for the bounty. By the end of three years, his reputation earned him the job of government lion hunter.

In his 1953 autobiography, *Cougar Killer*, Bruce wrote that he went on seven thousand lion hunts, killed nearly seven hundred lions and faced a different set of circumstances each time. The work was hard and dangerous. Due to his lame hand, Bruce used a handgun instead of a rifle. Once, when his Luger jammed as a lion charged him, Bruce fell backward, kicking at the cat while his hounds bit and pulled at its hind end. A swipe of the lion's paw ripped the sole off his boot. Luckily the dogs held the cat back long enough for Bruce to get his gun in working order and dispatch it. Another time his hounds cornered a lion but when Bruce went to shoot, nothing happened. Then he remembered his wife telling him that she'd unloaded his gun as she was worried one of the children would pick it up. While contemplating his options Bruce grabbed a dog to save it from the lion's claws and noticed two little bags of bullets tied to its collar.

It wasn't only the big cats that posed a danger. While chasing a lion through the bush in 1928 Bruce was jabbed in the eye by a sharp stick. He collapsed due to the severe pain but his fifteen-year-old son was the only person with him so, by force of will, he managed to finish the hunt. He spent three weeks in a hospital with both eyes tightly bandaged. "From that day on I knew I would be taking the risk of suffering a miserable, lingering death every time I went hunting alone, and this was most of the time...and in lonely, rugged areas," he confessed in *Cougar Killer*. Nonetheless, even though he was blind in one eye and had a crippled hand, Bruce continued to hunt cougars for another nineteen years.

When he wasn't hunting lions, Jay Bruce wrote articles for *Field & Stream* and *Outdoor Life*. He also starred in three movies.

The grainy black and white film of the last one, made circa 1924 with audio commentary added by Bruce twenty-nine years later, shows him bounding up mountains, fording chest-high rivers and scrambling down rock bluffs as he chased after his dogs on the trail of a mountain lion. No doubt he was showing off a bit for the filmmaker but it's obvious that Bruce was incredibly fit and strong. In 1953, accompanied by a live mountain lion, Bruce took this movie and his book on tour to New York, Chicago and other big cities.

Tom Phillips, Bruce's great-nephew, told me, "According to those who knew him, Jay was a difficult person to get along with. But when he came to town he was treated like a rock star and all the old folks in the county talked about going on a hunt with him or having a picture of him with a lion."

At one point in his career, Bruce began an experimental breeding program with some of his best dogs. He wanted them to "follow a cold trail silently, make a fast finish, tree lions and keep them treed for ten to twelve hours at a time barking constantly during all that time." He was so successful that the Canadian government ordered hounds from him. Bruce retired in 1947, and right up to his death at age eighty-one in 1963 he spoke fondly of the devotion of the canine cohorts of his working days and the companionship they provided.

Of course, not all cougar hunters had dogs specifically bred for the purpose. In the early bounty years on Vancouver Island any dog would do and many a collie, Airedale terrier, Labrador retriever and foxhound did a splendid job. John Cecil Smith's favourite cougar dog was a collie-spaniel cross called Dick. Only problem was, Dick belonged to Smith's older brother, Horace.

Financial difficulties brought the Smith family from England to central Vancouver Island in 1887, a time "when British Columbia had more cougars than bees," John told his second wife,

"Cougar" Smith was so soft-spoken and gentlemanly that most people were shocked to discover his occupation. He shot his first cougar at age fourteen and was renowned for his ability to track the big cats. In fact, some said he led his dogs to the cougars instead of the other way around. Smith, eighteen years old in this photo, had many cougar hounds over his forty years of hunting but his favourite, shown here, was a collie-spaniel cross called Dick. *Photo mcr009248 courtesy Museum at Campbell River*

Elinor Swain. The family's Black Creek farm wasn't fenced so nine-year-old Smith rounded up the milk cows each morning. He learned to watch for hoofprints in soft earth and to pay attention to trampled ferns. It wasn't long before he could tell which cow he was following and how it had spent its time in the woods. When Smith shot his first big cat at the age of fourteen he had no idea he'd eventually become a bounty hunter and a big game guide famous worldwide.

Vancouver Island was a logger's paradise and the lush growth found in clear-cuts resulted in an exploding deer population.

Cougar numbers also increased, perhaps to as many as four thousand by the early twentieth century, according to author Dell Hall. Inevitably, some of them added livestock to their menu. Farmers often didn't have the time, know-how or inclination to track the troublesome cats so they asked Smith to deal with any problems. He received the five-dollar bounty British Columbia paid for mature cats, which later rose to forty dollars. Word got around and it wasn't long before Smith was on twenty-four-hour call. Soon, big game hunters were hiring him as a guide. He was just twenty when he received a letter from a noted Austrian hunter addressed to "Cougar" Smith of Vancouver Island.

Smith married twice and had five children with his first wife. At different times he supplemented his hunting and guiding income by farming, logging, working as a fisheries inspector and selling cougar kittens he'd raised to zoos and game farms. In the early 1920s the provincial government hired him as a professional cougar hunter, which meant he received a salary as well as the bounty. To collect the bounty a hunter had to show the dead animal to a government official who punched a hole in its left ear and requisitioned payment. Afterward, Smith often sold the carcasses to Chinatown merchants in the nearby coal-mining community of Cumberland, the skins to taxidermists and the skulls to museums. He kept the tails for himself and was renowned for his cat-tail soup.

As well as having a reputation for being the most aggressive cougars, those on Vancouver Island were notoriously difficult to track. "The undergrowth—mostly salal—was so thick fellows used to joke about treeing a cougar in it," Dell Hall wrote in *Island Gold*. Smith's reputation as a tracker was legendary and many were convinced he could see in the dark. According to writer and naturalist Hamilton Mack Laing, Smith would disappear into the woods for days, and despite often being wet to the skin, he would only stop to build a fire and brew some tea. Food, blankets and even Smith's compass might be left behind but never his battered black kettle.

For many years Smith used an old Hudson's Bay musket. Rumour had it he never measured the powder, just put a handful in, rammed some newspaper on top and then threw in some shot. "To cougar hunt in the forest of Vancouver Island," Laing wrote, "a person must combine the travelling prowess of a bull moose, the back packing stamina of a burro and the scout craft of a leather-stocking. Cougar Smith is the best panther hunter on earth."

In *Beyond the City Limits*, Smith's daughter, Margaret Dunn, recalled that most of her dad's dogs were a mixed lot of part-bloodhounds, part-foxhounds, an English sheepdog and some whose ancestry was anyone's guess. Although most cougar hunters had a close relationship with their dogs, they tried not to get too attached. It could take a couple of years to train a hound and only a second to lose it to a cougar. But that didn't stop eighteen-year-old Smith from forming a strong bond with his brother's dog, Dick. Smith offered to buy Dick but Horace refused to sell. So, according to a story Smith often told later in life, he asked Horace to fork over the seventy dollars he owed him. Horace didn't have the money so Smith told his brother he could have the dog back when he repaid the loan.

As well as training dogs, on at least one occasion Smith trained a cougar hunter. English-born Roderick Haig-Brown first visited Canada's west coast in the 1920s. An avid sports fisherman, he eventually married and raised four children in Campbell River, where he became a magistrate, conservationist and award-winning author of twenty-five books. His first years in the country were spent working as a professional hunting guide and bounty hunter in the Nimpkish River area of northern Vancouver Island. Haig-Brown was twenty-two the winter he learned how to hunt cougars from fifty-eight-year-old Smith.

Cougar Hunter: A Memoir of Roderick Haig-Brown by Al Purdy contains a collection of letters that Purdy and Haig-Brown sent each other. In one, Haig-Brown described Smith as "lean and spare as a lodge pole pine." He recalled Smith bending over in the slash with his glasses sliding down his nose to pick out a strand of cougar fur on a log. "He'd track by eye as far as possible and then let the dogs loose when he thought they were really close. It was informed intuition over and over. My impression was that the dogs didn't lead Smith to the cougar...he led them. As a woodsman he was in a class by himself."

Haig-Brown's third book, *Panther*, is based on Smith and his hunting expertise. "He was pleasant to travel with and I admired him greatly," Haig-Brown wrote in a letter to Purdy. "We operated companionably, smoked rollies and talked freely. His perfect companionship in the woods under all sorts of conditions made the learning a very pleasant task." Many people were surprised when they met the slight and soft-spoken Smith. A Toronto journalist who interviewed him in 1937 wrote, "For a certainty, he doesn't look the part of a varmint slayer...A milder mannered, gentler soul than Cougar Smith never strolled through a forest or ran a marauding cougar to his doom."

The easygoing Smith was adamant about one thing. "I've heard people say cougars are cowardly creatures and I want to scotch that idea right here for it isn't so," he said in *The Nine Lives of Cougar Smith*, an unpublished manuscript written by his second wife, Elinor. "They are afraid of nothing but noise and that's the reason they'll tree for a pack of dogs and it's the only reason. They aren't afraid of a dog any more than I am. Cougars can be fearsome critters when you meet them under certain conditions. One or two had me pretty badly scared at different times." Smith quit chasing cougars in 1953 to spend more time in his garden and died eight years later at the age of eighty-three. It's estimated he killed more than a thousand cougars over a span of nearly sixty years.

During the bounty years cougars were hunted and killed by young and old, male and female. Most farm women weren't shy about shooting a cougar if it entered the yard. Some would even mount a horse and take after it if it was killing livestock. Others accompanied their husbands on hunts; some killed cougars for cash. Instead of tramping all over the country tracking with dogs, more than one woman lured the predators into her yard. Perhaps, with children and gardens to look after, women didn't have the option of taking off for long periods of time. Or maybe it just seemed like a more practical way of getting the job done.

Ada Annie Rae-Arthur, an educated woman who worked as a stenographer, became a bounty hunter by circumstance rather than choice. When her husband, Willie, took to drink and opium in a big way, a doctor advised removing him from temptation. Rae-Arthur was twenty-seven when she, Willie and their three children moved from Vancouver to the head of Hesquiat Harbour on the west coast of Vancouver Island in 1915. By 1931 they had eight more children. Sickly Willie looked after the house and kids, as well as making regular boat trips to Tofino for get-togethers with the "boys." In the meantime Rae-Arthur created a clearing in the rain forest, built drainage ditches and began planting. Over time, her garden grew to roughly three hectares (seven acres), and in addition to a prodigious vegetable plot contained fruit and decorative trees, including some exotic species from Asia, as well as tulips, daffodils, lilies, irises, peonies, two hundred varieties of dahlias and other flowers and shrubs.

After moving to the west coast of Vancouver Island, Cougar Annie created a nursery garden out of the wilderness, raised eleven children and outlived three husbands. She killed cougars for the bounty too. John Manning took this photograph in the early 1960s while working for the *Victoria Daily Times*. He showed up on Cougar Annie's doorstep unannounced and said she welcomed him warmly and discussed at length her appetite for killing cougars. *Photo C-04904 by John Manning, courtesy Royal BC Museum, BC Archives*

In *Cougar Annie's Garden* Margaret Horsfield described a small woman with work roughened hands who did whatever was necessary to keep her family going. A room in the house was converted into a small store and post office and Rae-Arthur sold plants through the mail. She also raised chickens, goats, rabbits and geese.

Hats were her one indulgence and her standard gardening outfit consisted of a long dress, a fashionable hat and gumboots. When Willie died in 1936 Rae-Arthur soon realized she couldn't look after the children, house, garden and various business ventures by herself. So she advertised for a husband. Over the years she married three more times, the last union taking place when Rae-Arthur was seventy-two and her spouse sixty, making her a pioneer in the modern use of the term "cougar." All the men predeceased her and rumours abounded that she murdered at least one of them.

Rae-Arthur was a crack shot and it made sense to take advantage of the cougar bounty but she was much too busy to go hunting. Instead she used her goats as bait. Horsfield recounted in detail how Rae-Arthur placed three bear traps around the property—one a scant nine metres (thirty feet) away from the house. They were covered during the day when the goats and children were out and "Beware Cougar Trap" signs were posted for unwary visitors. Come nightfall, Rae-Arthur uncovered the traps and sometimes tethered a goat nearby. She often slept in her clothes, jumping up and running outside with her rifle as soon as the goat began to bleat.

Once a cougar got into the barn and killed nine goats. Rae-Arthur set her traps and baited them with pieces of one of the slaughtered goats. On the second night she heard noises and rushed out to find the cougar caught by two toes. When the cat saw her it tried to escape, and when that failed it lunged toward her. "I sighted fast and shot," she said later. "He staggered and fell eight feet from me." Another time she chased a cougar into the woods with her flashlight. "He had dragged a goat quite a way into the forest, heavy as it was. I saw him, though. He was hiding down near a stump atop the goat, he saw me too, and was just ready to spring. His mouth was wide open. I don't usually shoot in the mouth but I could see this would go down his throat. I shot quickly. He dropped on the spot and rolled back."

A cougar once knocked Rae-Arthur down but she saved herself by screaming loudly. Cougar Annie didn't win every encounter. One year a cougar killed all her goats, leaving the family without milk. Indeed, the size of the goat herd went up and down depending on the deer population. If there were plenty of deer for cougars to dine on she might have forty goats; a decade later there might only be three.

As with most bounty hunters, the number of animals Rae-Arthur actually killed is open to debate. A realistic figure is probably seventy. In 1955 she claimed the bounty on ten, earning four hundred dollars. And even though cataracts made it difficult to see, she shot a cougar on her seventy-third birthday. She skinned the animals herself and sold the hides for extra money. As for the meat, she fed some to the chickens and canned and ate the rest. By the time Rae-Arthur was eighty, she could hardly see and had lost most of her teeth, energy and strength. Even so, she remained at Hesquiat Harbour until 1983, dying two years later, at age ninety-six, in the Port Alberni hospital.

Cougar Annie wasn't the only woman to gain fame as a cougar killer. Over on the British Columbia mainland, everybody thought Bergie Solberg was just a peculiar character living in the bush until a French crew showed up to film *The Cougar Lady of the Sunshine Coast*. Bergilot Solberg moved from Norway to Canada with her parents and younger sister, Minnie, in 1926 when she was three years old. Her dad built a four-room house in Sechelt Inlet, about sixty kilometres (thirty-seven miles) in a straight line northwest from Vancouver on the mainland coast. He worked as a hand logger and taught his daughters how to hunt and trap. When they were older they helped him log. The girls were home-schooled

Bergie Solberg lived most of her life in a remote bay on Sechelt Inlet in British Columbia. Well educated in the ways of the woods, she earned a living by logging, trapping and hunting cougars. She liked cowboy hats and yodelling and kept several dogs for company, all named Bush. *Photo courtesy the Alsgard family, Sechelt Community Archives*

and although they may have possessed only a rudimentary level of reading and writing skills, they were well educated in the ways of the land.

Minnie married and moved to Jervis Inlet; Bergie lived with her parents until they died. In her younger years she worked in logging camps blowing whistles, setting chokers and pulling straw line. Solberg raised chickens and goats and usually had several dogs, all named Bush, to keep her company. In her spare time she liked to play the guitar, sing and yodel. Solberg used her dad's homemade wooden boat to go to Sechelt once a month for supplies. Her going-to-town attire consisted of western-style shirts, a battered purple cowboy hat and a big buck knife on a belt. It's said she was a hard worker and very strong. She often competed at the Sechelt community's loggers' sports days and in 1976 was proclaimed Lady Logger of the Day.

Solberg operated a trapline for more than fifty years, selling mink, raccoon and other animal pelts for cash. She hunted bears and cougars too. Several times she was taken to court for shooting a bear out of season, letting her trapping licence expire or using her traps illegally. She often claimed she couldn't read, using that as an excuse for breaking the law. The conservation officer was always trying to make her see the error of her ways, however, and once tried to confiscate her rifle for shooting a cougar out of season. They wrestled over the weapon and although Solberg won she complained about a sore shoulder for weeks afterward. Like Rae-Arthur, Solberg's goats served two purposes: milk to drink and bait to lure cougars in close. As far as Solberg was concerned, cougars were made for one purpose: to shoot and skin, so she could sell the hide. She preferred venison but ate cougar meat once in a while, and said, "It tastes okay, kind of sweet."

In the story "Bergie Solberg: Cougar Lady of the Sunshine Coast," Ken Collins has written about a hunting expedition he went on with Solberg when she was in her late sixties. "Just like a bear, Bergie would put her head down, hunch her shoulders, and push her way through the dense underbrush." As she raced across the landscape, only stopping to slurp goat's milk out of a quart canning jar, Solberg pointed out various tracks to Collins. Then she found some cougar scat. "Like a connoisseur rolling a favoured Cuban cigar with the fingers, she fondled the piece of feces, broke it in half, and put it to her nose, inhaling deeply," Collins wrote. Then she told him that the scat was fresh, what the cougar had eaten, when it had defecated and which way it was travelling.

Even though she was getting on in years, Solberg refused to move to town, saying it would kill her. Concerned about her isolation, a friend set up a CB radio so she could communicate with the outside world. He gave her the handle "Cougar Lady." When she didn't respond to a call on November 11, 2002, someone went to investigate and found the eighty-year-old dead from a stroke. Although it's estimated Solberg only killed twenty cougars, her reputation spread beyond Sechelt via the French film and a segment on CBC Television's *The Golden Years*.

In some ways, bounty hunters and early government predator control agents were the last vestiges of the "man against the wilderness" era of the Old West. Many were specialists in their fields and frequently provided a valuable service to those experiencing cougar predation; they were often quirky characters, too. And they usually performed their work out of sight of others, making it easy for tall tales to reach gigantic proportions over time.

For more than two hundred years some form of cougar bounty was practised in Canada and the US. One of the earliest eastern states to introduce a payment for killing cougars was Connecticut in 1684. Out west it was the Oregon Territories in 1864. But while eastern and midwestern portions of the continent had low or no cougar populations by the mid- to late 1800s, the big cats managed to hold their ground in the west. New Mexico ended its cougar bounty in 1923, followed by British Columbia in 1957. From that point on, one or more western states and provinces stopped paying bounties on cougars each year, with the last being Arizona in 1970. By then it was obvious that the bounty was an expensive and ineffective way for governments to manage cougars.

Besides, so many of the big cats had been killed that livestock predation was not the problem it had been in the past. Records indicate that 12,461 mountain lions were destroyed during California's bounty years, and in *Island Gold* Dell Hall calculated that 21,871 cougars were killed by bounty hunters in BC. Despite being heavily hunted for an extended period of time, cougars were lucky. Perhaps because they're so rarely seen and so labour intensive to chase, they weren't at the top of the bounty hit list. Wolves and grizzly bear populations were extirpated (became locally extinct) in some areas of the west while the cougar managed to survive. But even before the bounty was cancelled, humans were chasing cougars as a form of recreation.

CHAPTER 5:
A Change in Attitude

The big horse killing cat...with a
heart both craven and cruel.

—THEODORE ROOSEVELT,
A Book-Lover's Holiday in the Open

By the turn of the twentieth century, cougars were being hunted for sport as well as bounty. Theodore Roosevelt, one of the most well-known big game hunters in North America, was renowned for his hunting escapades and lived up to his reputation when it came to bagging his first cougar. As he once wrote to his thirteen-year-old son: "After a couple of hundred yards, the dogs caught him, and a great fight followed. They could have killed him by themselves, but he bit or clawed four of them, and for fear he might kill one I ran in and stabbed him behind the shoulder, thrusting the knife you loaned me right into his heart. I have always wished to kill a cougar as I did this one, with dogs and the knife." The letter, eventually published in *Theodore Roosevelt's Letters to His Children*, was dated January 14, 1901.

Roosevelt, who later that year would become the twenty-sixth president of the United States, had just finished a five-week hunting trip with guide Johnny B. Goff at the Keystone Ranch in Colorado. They'd bagged fourteen cougars in all. The largest—the one Roosevelt killed with a knife—weighed 103 kilograms (227 pounds) and was 2.5 metres (8 feet) long. Roosevelt was ecstatic. He'd been keen on cougars for some time but had never seen one up close before.

By today's standards, Roosevelt's hunting expedition would be deemed a cruel and needless massacre. But it took place in another time with different beliefs and long before modern methods of studying wildlife were available. Roosevelt considered his write-up of the hunt, published in 1905 as *Outdoor Pastimes of an American Hunter*, "the first reasonably full and trustworthy life history of the cougar as regards its most essential details."

Born in New York City on October 27, 1858, Roosevelt experienced poor health as a child and had such severe asthma he had to be home-schooled in his early years. He loved natural history, however, and at age eight saw a dead seal at a market, obtained the head and, with a couple of buddies, formed a kids' club called the Roosevelt Museum of Natural History. After graduating from Harvard he was diagnosed with a heart condition and advised to

Poor health as a child and a heart condition didn't prevent Theodore Roosevelt from becoming a robust outdoorsman and one of the most well-known big game hunters in North America. He killed his first cougar with a knife and, as the twenty-sixth president of the United States, set aside large parcels of land for national parks and became involved in the conservation movement. *Photo courtesy Library of Congress Prints and Photographs Division Washington, DC, Bain Collection*

get a desk job. Instead, Roosevelt opted to follow what he called "a strenuous life," which included boxing, polo, judo and a variety of other activities such as horseback riding, hunting and skinny-dipping in the Potomac River in the winter. Through determination and a vigorous lifestyle the sickly kid transformed himself into a robust, barrel-chested man.

As well as being deeply involved in politics and an avid outdoorsman, Roosevelt was a prolific writer who documented his hunting exploits in numerous articles and books. Reading these accounts it's obvious that like many hunters, Roosevelt loved the physical and mental stimulation of hunting cougars and relished the excitement of the chase more than the fatal shot.

Stories about sports hunting can be traced back to ancient Egypt and Babylonia, where royalty of both sexes enjoyed the adventure of pursuing large land animals. On occasion dogs, or captive panthers and leopards, were used to flush and chase game. It's said that European and British nobility looked forward to hunting almost as much as engaging in battle, and that they viewed tracking and killing big game excellent hands-on training for warfare. In Canada and the US hunting was initially a way to obtain food for the table and to earn a living by acquiring furs to trade. With the advent of agriculture and animal husbandry, people began eliminating predators that interfered with their ability to provide for themselves, and the introduction of the bounty system added a cash incentive to the defence of private property. Toward the end of the nineteenth century, as a portion of the population found themselves with more leisure time, money and easy access to wilderness areas, killing big game for pleasure became more common.

But even before sports hunting became popular, cougars were sometimes exploited for "sporting" purposes. In *California Grizzly,*

Tracy Irwin Storer and Lloyd Pacheco Tevis related how bears were pitted against bulls and occasionally cougars in arenas. A witness to an 1865 fight in Castroville, California, said the cougar leapt onto the grizzly's back and reached around to rake its eyes and nose with its claws. The bear kept rolling over to remove the cat from its back but every time it regained its feet, the cougar attacked again. Cougars and bears don't get along at the best of times—it's not unheard of for a bear to drive a cougar off its kill or scavenge the carcass, and the two predators kill each other's young on occasion. No mention is made of whether the Castroville incident was a fight to the death, but the cougar was declared the winner of the bout.

As sports hunting increased in popularity, men and sometimes women hunted deer, bighorn sheep, bears, wolves, cougars and other large game, gaining prestige for bagging the biggest horns or heaviest animal. Skins were tanned and displayed and heads, antlers and sometimes entire bodies were mounted as trophies. And there was an extra thrill in hunting and killing animals that were difficult to locate and potentially dangerous to confront.

Indiscriminate hunting, along with the ongoing increase in human population and changes to the terrain due to settlements, ranches and farms, resulted in a dramatic decrease in ungulate populations. Now, in addition to viewing cougars as a threat to livestock, hunters also saw them as competitors for big game. Sports hunting clubs had formed as early as the 1830s but in the late 1800s organizations across the continent began lobbying governments to pass laws to regulate hunting and increase predator control.

In 1906, as president of the United States, Theodore Roosevelt established the Grand Canyon National Game Preserve on the Kaibab Plateau in Arizona, to protect "the finest deer herd in America." Ranging across what is now the North Rim of Grand Canyon National Park, the mule deer in the region sported record-breaking large antlers. "The preservation of game and of wild life generally—aside from the noxious species—on these reserves is of incalculable benefit to the people as a whole," wrote Roosevelt in *A Book-Lover's Holiday in the Open*. "As the game increases in these national refuges and nurseries it overflows into the surrounding country. Very wealthy men can have private game-preserves of their own. But the average man of small or moderate means can enjoy the vigorous pastime of the chase, and, indeed, can enjoy wild nature, only if there are good general laws, properly enforced, for the preservation of the game and wildlife, and if there are big parks or reserves provided for the use of all our people, like those of the Yellowstone, the Yosemite, and the Colorado."

Hunting was banned in the Kaibab and a vigorous extermination program to eliminate the plateau of all predators, especially cougars and coyotes, was launched. James T. Owen, alternately called "Uncle Jimmy" or "Cougar Killer of the Kaibab," was appointed game warden for the area. It's said that in his twelve-year tenure he killed anywhere from three hundred to more than six hundred cougars. Roosevelt, who accompanied Owen on several hunts, wrote, "They [cougars] are the most successful of all still-hunters, killing deer much more easily than a wolf can; and those we killed were very fat. Their every movement is so lithe and stealthy, they move with such sinuous and noiseless caution, and are such past masters in the art of concealment, that they are hardly ever seen unless roused by dogs."

And sure enough, as predators were killed, the number of mule deer increased. In 1906 the deer population of the Kaibab was estimated at four thousand. Aldo Leopold, an author and scientist sometimes called "the father of wildlife ecology," later determined that the carrying capacity of the region at that time would have been around thirty thousand. But by 1919, the year the Grand Canyon became a national park, forest officials worried that burgeoning deer herds would eventually destroy all vegetation on the plateau. In typical fashion, governments and bureaucracies had different opinions on both the problem and appropriate ways to deal with it. Many felt the situation didn't require immediate attention and, perhaps more importantly, deer watching had become a primary tourist draw for the park and no one wanted to jeopardize that.

By 1924 the deer population had grown to one hundred thousand and the ungulates had stripped the land of all edible foliage up to a height of 2.5 metres (8 feet). The area was opened for deer hunting but estimates suggest that over the next two years as many as sixty thousand deer starved to death. By 1931 the number of deer had dwindled to twenty thousand, and eight years later less than ten thousand were still alive.

The Kaibab fiasco and similar predator control programs were sharp reminders of what can happen when humans disrupt the complex balance of nature. It's now known that while cougars can pose serious threats to isolated and endangered herds of elk, caribou and bighorn sheep, in most situations they don't decimate deer populations. Instead, they keep the ungulates a little bit on edge, which means they're constantly moving from one place to the next and don't over-browse any one location.

Popular western writer Zane Grey summed up the situation in his book *The Deer Stalker*, which tells the story of the 1924 attempt to save the starving Kaibab deer by driving them to another area. Grey participated in the event and his fictionalized rendition is supposed to be fairly accurate. One of his characters, Jim Evans, is based on "Uncle Jimmy" Owen, the hunter hired to kill predators on the plateau. In one chapter Evans explains that humans have upset the balance of nature by "killin' off the varmints, specially the cougars." The fictional hunter continues, "These heah deer ain't had nothin' to check their overbreedin' an' inbreedin.'"

But even before the Kaibab disaster, a subtle shift in the way people thought about the land and the animals inhabiting it was taking place. Some wondered if, rather than exploiting the wilderness and its resources without thought, humankind might be better served if the natural world was preserved for future generations. And that perhaps people, animals and the environment were not separate entities, but were intrinsically linked so that what happened to one eventually affected the others.

John James Audubon shared this point of view. In 1803, at age eighteen, he emigrated from Haiti to America, where he studied and painted birds on his family's estate near Philadelphia. Audubon spent hours in the field observing birds and, like his contemporaries, shot specimens so he could examine them in detail. His goal was to record all bird species in North America. But contrary to the usual practice of painting wildlife in formal, ridgid poses, Audubon placed them in life-like positions surrounded by elements of their natural habitat. His 1827 publication *The Birds of America*, frequently cited as one of the finest ornithological books in the world, presented the public with a more holistic view of nature than many had been exposed to in the past.

Award-winning illustrator and author Ernest Thompson Seton increasingly decried the mass killing of cougars. Seton believed that creatures had wants and feelings similar to humans and, as such, had rights as well. In 1909 he wrote, "Of all that has been written or is known of the American cougar...fully ninety-nine percent deals with how we may hunt, pursue, murder and destroy this wonderful beautiful animal. Of the one percent remaining, about one-half deals with alleged more or less doubtful attacks of this splendid creature on man...'Kill, kill, kill' is their cry…fifty pages there are of senseless, brutal killing and only one of 'Stop.'"

Another writer who sided with cougars was Charles G.D. Roberts. Born in New Brunswick in 1860, Roberts worked as a teacher, editor, English professor and, eventually, full-time writer. After his poetry, Roberts was most well-known for his animal stories that, like Seton's, presented the narrative from the animals' point of view. Author Lyn Hancock has pointed out that his 1895 short story "Do Seek Their Meat from God" may be the first published Canadian fiction to feature a cougar. In the tale, a male and a female cougar are having trouble finding food due to settlers' impact on the countryside. They come across a small child and are about to attack it when they are killed by a man passing by. The man later finds two cougar cubs dead from starvation.

When Roberts wrote "They are but seeking with the strength, the cunning, the deadly swiftness given them to that end, the food convenient for them," he presented cougars not as wanton killers but as creatures doing only what is necessary to survive. "Do Seek Their Meat from God" also brings up a dilemma still discussed today: when people move into or alter an animal's habitat, are they justified in killing the animal when it follows its natural instincts?

These artists and writers and others like John Muir, Henry David Thoreau and Charles Darwin encouraged people to think of wild animals and nature from a different point of view. In turn, they were supported in their endeavours by book publishers, magazine editors and art galleries. But even as they were laying the groundwork for the early conservation movement, they were also revealing just how little scientific information about North American wildlife was available. Some common misconceptions about cougars were that they never attacked humans unless defending their cubs,

Stealthy and silent, cougars are rarely seen even by people who work in wilderness areas. Part of the reason is their colouring, which allows them to blend in with any landscape. And their huge padded paws mean they can creep up on prey without a sound.

that they killed prey and hauled it up a tree to eat it, and that they mated for life and raised their young together.

As it became apparent that Canada and the US did not contain an endless supply of wildlife, conservation became an increasingly popular topic. In addition to providing tips on how to bag a big buck or which fly was favoured by rainbow trout, articles in periodicals such as *Field & Stream* began covering the dwindling populations of some species. The late 1800s and early 1900s also saw the formation of numerous wildlife organizations, such as the Sierra Club, the Wildlife Conservation Society and the Audubon Society.

Long before the days of sophisticated equipment like radio telemetry collars, motion sensor trail cameras or GPS units, a common way to research wildlife was to shoot it and skin it or stuff it so the skull, skeleton and hides or feathers could be examined at leisure. In May 1922 the National Collection of Heads and Horns opened "In Memory of the Vanishing Big Game of the World," at the Bronx Zoo in New York. According to a *New York Times* article, the specimens were "either presented by the sportsmen who shot them, or purchased with funds contributed by men and women keenly interested in wild animals and public education along zoological lines."

Roosevelt donated numerous samples he'd collected on big game expeditions. In fact, for many years the skull of the big cat he killed on his 1901 Colorado hunting trip held the world's record for size. A year after Heads and Horns opened, Roosevelt, George Bird Grinnell, editor of *Forest and Stream* magazine, and other associates formed the Boone and Crockett Club, to "promote the conservation and management of wildlife, especially big game, and its habitat, to preserve and encourage hunting and to maintain the highest ethical standards of fair chase and sportsmanship in North America."

Like any change in consciousness, the concept of conservation took a while to catch on. Despite being extirpated in eastern Canada and the US, many years passed before cougars were recognized as anything other than vermin. Gradually, bounty programs were phased out, cougars were classified as big game animals and hunting seasons, bag limits and regulations were introduced. But even some who hunted the big cats for recreation or profit were beginning to reconsider the ethics of their behaviour.

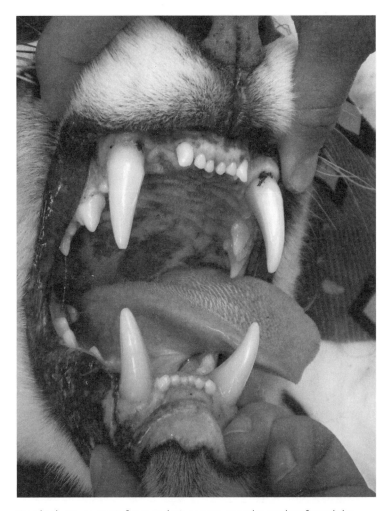

One look at a cougar's fangs and it's easy to see why settlers feared the big cats as man-eating beasts. But as more information became available, people began to value the predator's role in the environment. This 82-kilogram (180-pound) male was the first cougar captured and collared in the Cypress Hills Interprovincial Park in Alberta and Saskatchewan. He was around six years old when this photo was taken in 2008. A year later he died with his ribs kicked in, leading researchers from the University of Alberta to speculate that he'd been killed attempting to take down an elk. *Photo by Michelle Bacon*

Zane Grey grew up in Zanesville, Ohio, which had been founded by his maternal great-grandfather. Baseball, writing and fishing
were his passions. He attended the University of Pennsylvania on a
baseball scholarship but, to be practical, graduated in 1896 with a
degree in dentistry. After an invitation to hunt lions with Charles
Jesse "Buffalo" Jones, Grey ditched his dental drill and began
churning out fiction and non-fiction western adventure books. The
"burly shouldered, bronzed faced and grim" Buffalo Jones served as
a template for many of Grey's fictional protagonists, but in *Roping
American Lions in the Grand Canyon* he served up the real deal. In
it Grey tells the story of his 1908 trip with Jones and how they
and three other men chased lions up and down escarpments and
across Powell's Plateau. According to Grey they "stumbled on a
lion home, the breeding place of hundreds of lions," as well as lion
runways littered with hundreds of deer carcasses. The terrain was
rough. At times the men were forced to lower the dogs over cliffs
on ropes and rappel down after them. Despite the rigours of the
hunt Grey always hoped it wouldn't end too soon, "because the
race was too splendid a thing to cut short."

Buffalo Jones, sixty-four years old at the time, was known for
his ability to rope live lions. After the dogs treed a cat, he'd climb
up after it with a length of rope on a long stick. While the cat
snarled and hissed, he'd loop the rope over the lion's head with
the stick and yell, "Pull!" One or more of the men below would
do so and soon the lion would be hanging over a branch. It was
then slowly lowered far enough to tie its paws, jam a stick behind
the canine teeth and wrap some wire around the muzzle. After a
lion was secured, its bound paws were slung over a pole and it was
packed back to camp. There it was tied to a tree along with other
prizes of the hunt. On one expedition Buffalo Jones's crew had

six waiting to be transported to zoos. The lions constantly snarled and twisted against their restraints, determined to get away.

One time Grey leaned toward a bound lion until its face was only 15 centimetres (6 inches) from his. "He promptly spat on me," Grey wrote in *Roping American Lions in the Grand Canyon.*

> *"I had to steel my nerve to keep so close. But I wanted to see a wild lion's eyes at close range. They were exquisitely beautiful, their physical properties as wonderful as their expression. Great globes of tawny amber, streaked with delicate wavy lines of black, surrounding pupils of intense purple fire. Pictures shone and faded in the amber light—the shaggy tipped plateau, the dark pines and smoky canyons, the great dotted downward slopes, the yellow cliffs and crags. Deep in those live pupils, changing, quickening with a thousand vibrations, quivered the soul of this savage beast, the wildest of all wild Nature, unquenchable love of life and freedom, flame of defiance and hate."*

Grey wasn't the only person to be mesmerized by a cougar's eyes; Roosevelt described them as "two discs of pure gold," and after a close encounter Frank Hibben recalled "the burning green eyes I will see in nightmares for the rest of my life."

At the end of Grey's book the men seized Sultan, a legendary lion and the largest any of them had ever seen. But before his paws could be tied, Sultan leapt over a precipice and, because he was so heavy, strangled before the men could pull him up. That's when Jones announced he'd never rope another lion. In his 1924 introduction to the book Grey said he hoped readers would find "more than mere entertainment" and that the stories of lions would "generate the impulse which may help to preserve our great outdoors for future generations."

As well as sharing Grey's love of fishing and writing, author and magistrate Roderick Haig-Brown echoed his sentiments regarding wildlife and nature. In the preface of an edition of *Panther,* the Campbell River, BC, resident wrote,

> *"During the course of the research for the book I became re-luctant to kill cougars and started to follow and check their movements simply by visual tracking…the most important new thing to come from [recent] sophisticated research is the firm establishment of the fact that cougars have a proper and valuable place in the ecology of deer and elk ranges…many of us believed something of the sort even as long as 40 years ago, and were arguing against strong opposition for the abolition of bounty killing.*
>
> *"We were aware that cougars, like most wild animals, seldom kill wastefully and that when they did there was always some explanation," he continued. "A few aberrant individuals may become too dangerous to domestic livestock or even to humans and these should be promptly hunted down and removed to protect the reputation of the species as a whole."*

Haig-Brown's increasing awareness of nature as a valuable and fragile entity led him to write about and give talks on the topic throughout Canada and the US. "What is the nature of man in relation to his environment?" he wrote. "Can he become sensitive, generous and considerate to his world and the other creatures that share it, or is his nature rooted in blood, sex and darkness?"

Haig-Brown wrote *Panther* in 1934. Eight years later, Walt Disney Productions released *Bambi.* Although the animated film failed to make money in its initial box office release and raised the ire of big game hunters, it is recognized as a classic depiction

Cougars are popular mascots for university sports teams. In the past it wasn't unusual for the big cats to be kept in cages on campus and toured around sports fields during breaks in the game. Today, the University of Houston is probably the only school to have a live cougar as a mascot. The cub shown here was one of three orphaned kittens. His siblings were quickly rescued but Shasta VI, as he's now called, remained hidden until a biologist gave a cougar-like chirp. Shasta VI lives at the Houston Zoo and appears at UH events via a webcam. *Photo courtesy the University of Houston Alumni Association and the Houston Zoo, Inc.*

of heartless humans threatening wildlife. And there's no doubt the film influenced many; even former Beatle Paul McCartney once said the death of Bambi's mother was the catalyst for his interest in animal rights. By the 1960s the building momentum of the environmental movement had spilled over into mainstream society. Saving wildlife and natural areas was the cool thing to do.

As the cougar acquired varying levels of protection, the secretive cat also gained increasing cachet as a sign of status and prestige. Advertising gurus have long taken advantage of the cat's allure and many a tawny feline has been paired with a sleek model to catch the consumer's eye. Most folks are familiar with the Mercury Cougar automobile and PUMA brand sportswear. Other items ranging from handguns to bourbon and beer also bear the name cougar. Even Apple got into the act with a Mountain Lion operating system.

Research for this book included setting up a Google Alert for "cougars" to keep informed about studies, sightings and encounters. To my surprise, ninety percent or more of the links Google sent my way were related to university and college sports teams. The second most frequent "cougar" story was about older women dating or marrying younger men. Despite being controversial, this modern form of cougar culture has become big business, featuring puma parties and cougar clubs and contests.

But as much as cougars have become an icon of all that is sexy, strong and fierce, it's important to not forget that the actual animal is unpredictable and potentially dangerous, whether it's encountered in the wilderness, viewed in a roadside zoo or introduced as someone's pet.

CHAPTER 6:
Captive Cougars

There's no such thing as a tame cougar.

—ROBYN BARFOOT, curator, Cougar Mountain Zoo

"The owner went into the [African] lions' cage first, there were maybe three or four of them," Rick James recalled. "The lions growled and snarled and he really had to pay attention. He used a whip and chair to keep them back. It was scary to watch as a kid—you knew if he glanced away for a second they'd be on top of him.

"After that he'd go into the cougar cage," James continued. "They were laying in a bunk bed arrangement. As soon as the cougars saw the man they'd roll over on their backs and he'd rub their bellies. Then the cougars would put their front legs and paws around his shoulders and neck and lick his face. They were like big tame pussy cats compared to the lions."

The James family often visited Hertel Zoo when passing through Nanaimo, BC. But what stands out most in Rick James's mind is the time in 1956 when he was nine years old and got to hold one of the young cougars. "It was heavy, all squirming muscle and gristle. And even as a kitten, so strong and powerful."

Rick James will never forget holding a five- to six-month-old cougar cub at Hertel Zoo in 1956. But while he struggled to hang on to the squirming animal, it focused its attention on his younger sister, Bonnie. *Photo courtesy Rick James*

The zoo was popular with many families and Paul Hertel always put on a good show. But tragedy struck in May 1958 when an African lion escaped and killed a young girl playing in the nearby woods. The zoo was closed and Hertel was charged with manslaughter. He wasn't convicted but the jury recommended British Columbia establish regulations for the operation of private zoos.

Humans have kept wild animals since ancient times. Originally called menageries, early collections belonged to royalty and were primarily for their private use. King Solomon, William the Conqueror and China's Empress Tanki were all known to keep a variety of large cats, elephants, monkeys, birds and other exotic creatures. In the New World, Montezuma, emperor of the Aztecs, included pumas among his captive wild beasts. And ancient South American artwork often featured jaguars and cougars sitting next to people. Many of these private collections of wild animals ultimately became zoological gardens open to the public. Later, resourceful individuals took caged wildlife on the road as travelling exhibits.

In Canada and the US, hunters and farmers sometimes trapped and displayed bears, cougars and other animals for a small fee. Eventually exotic animals from overseas were imported, thus introducing mobile menageries and circuses to the continent. Many of these enterprises were small; others, such as the Ringling Bros. and Barnum & Bailey Circus, initially billed as the "World's Greatest Menagerie," gained worldwide reputations. North America's first official zoo opened in Halifax, Nova Scotia, in 1847.

Although some criticize the concept of zoos, they are the only way many people will ever see some wild and exotic animals in person. And an accredited zoo is a huge improvement over the old shoot and stuff it method of studying wildlife that was predominant in former times. As for animals born in zoos or orphaned in the wild while too young to survive on their own, a zoo can mean the difference between life and death.

Miksa, Keira and Tika were born in a Wisconsin zoo on May 20, 2011, and moved to Cougar Mountain Zoo in Issaquah, Washington, when they were eleven days old. Situated on just over three hectares (eight acres) the zoo is a small, intimate facility housing approximately one hundred animals. The non-profit society is funded by admissions, membership fees and donations. When I visited in March 2012, the nine-month-old cougars still had remnants of their spots. Miksa's coat was a striking shade of red while his sisters' coats were a more sombre grey. Their paws and forelegs were already huge in relation to the rest of their bodies and it was easy to see the power in their long rear legs, so clearly built for leaping and bounding. Their small, rounded ears constantly rotated to pick up sounds. As I watched, the trio amused themselves by sunbathing, roughhousing with each other and surreptitiously keeping an eye on the folks watching them.

Miksa, Keira and Tika play king of the mountain at Cougar Mountain Zoo in Issaquah, Washington. Shown here at nine months old, they've lived at the zoo since they were eleven days old. Most cougar siblings part ways when around two years old but since these three don't need to compete for food or other cougars to mate with, they'll remain close companions throughout their lives. *Photo by Robyn Barfoot*

At one point, Keira suddenly whipped around to stare intently at the other side of the compound. The focus and concentration was palpable. I moved to see what had caught the cat's attention and there, at the other end of the enclosure, was a small child. Every time one of the cougars saw a child the cat locked its eyes on the youngster, tracking them until they were out of sight. Children's small size, erratic movements and high-pitched voices make them look like prey to cougars. I later learned that zoo staff ask youngsters not to run within view of the cougar compound as the movement excites the cats' chase instinct. And when I asked Robyn Barfoot, the zoo curator, why a cougar was fixated on a volunteer sweeping the walkway, she explained that the person's downcast eyes and slightly bent position made them appear vulnerable.

Miksa spent most of his time as close to the people side of the enclosure as he could get. Although he didn't make eye contact, he frequently emitted a soft coughing sound. I thought he had a cold but it turns out chuffing is a way cougars communicate with each other and, in this case, nearby humans, sort of a big kitty way of saying hello. The only other sound the siblings made was a bird-like chirping, the standard "Hi" or "Where are you?" call between siblings, and with their mother (or in this case familiar zoo staff or visitors). Other than that, the cats were totally silent; their oversized padded paws made absolutely no sound even when they were running or playing. Once—from a complete standstill—Tika leapt about 1.5 metres (5 feet) high and the same distance across, clearing a bush and her sister along the way. The entire motion was graceful, agile and eerily soundless.

At the time the two females weighed approximately 29.5 kilograms (65 pounds) each while their brother—males typically weigh thirty percent more than females—tipped the scale at 38.5 kilograms (85 pounds). "That's 85 cougar pounds," explained big cat specialist Robyn Barfoot. "That means a lot of muscle. Pound for pound, cougars are the most powerful of the big cats. They can take down an animal ten times their body weight while a lion or tiger only kills prey three to four times their weight."

Barfoot fell in love with large felines after watching world-renowned animal trainer and circus performer Gunther Gebel-Williams in a Ringling Bros. and Barnum & Bailey Circus act when she was four years old. In 2005, after working at several zoos and completing a stint of tiger conservation in India, Barfoot was employed by Cougar Mountain Zoo; she became general curator the following year.

The life of a cougar in the wild is violent and fraught with danger. Adults of both sexes are preoccupied with finding prey and mating. Females expend a lot of energy raising their young while males fight amongst themselves over mates and territory and are often battle-scarred. Disease and dental problems are common and it's not unusual for kittens to die from starvation or to be killed and eaten by predators including adult male cougars. And sometimes the cats are hit by vehicles or shot by humans. The average lifespan of a wild cougar is eight to twelve years; well-cared-for captive cougars often live until eighteen or twenty, with one resident of Big Cat Rescue in Tampa, Florida, dying just short of its thirtieth birthday.

Cougars are excellent hunters, but obtaining food is a risky undertaking. The cats are chased off their kills by bears, wolves or more dominant cougars and are sometimes injured or even killed while attempting to take down prey. In March 2012, people travelling along Highway 93 near Radium Hot Springs in southwestern BC witnessed a jumble of rocks and snow cascading down a cliff in Sinclair Canyon. At the centre of the avalanche a cougar rode the back of a bighorn sheep, jaws tightly clamped on its throat. When the duo slid to a stop at the end of a more than ten-metre (thirty-three-foot) drop, the cougar, perhaps disturbed by the traffic, walked away. While the sheep was mortally wounded and had to be put down, the cougar tackled and killed another bighorn sheep the following day.

In contrast, Miksa, Keira and Tika lead a pampered existence. They romp in a large compound with a dirt, sand and grass floor and real trees and rocks. There are logs and a towering boulder mound to climb, a couple of caves to hide in and heated platforms to curl up on. Like house cats, cougars may nap as much as eighteen hours a day. Zoo cougars also get regular vet check-ups. The three cats at Cougar Mountain Zoo don't get an opportunity to hunt, of course, but Tika, the smallest yet feistiest of the lot, killed and ate a bird that flew into the compound and defended the carcass from her siblings until she was ready to give it up. Zoo cougars are fed a manufactured diet that includes marrow, muscle meat and blood—just what they'd eat in the wild. And since free-roaming cougars don't eat every day, the three fast once a week. After their permanent teeth came in, they were given bones to gnaw on. They also get occasional treats in the way of venison, salmon and steak donated by zoo members and volunteers.

"It's been my experience that cougars aren't big on pork," noted Barfoot. "And they don't like tongue. Heart and liver seem to be the main attraction for them, then the kidneys." These preferences make sense as organ meats are packed with nutrients and the heart and liver are the part of a carcass wild cougars generally consume first.

In nature cougars are constantly on the move searching for prey, finding a mate or defending their territory. Cougar Mountain Zoo employees keep their charges stimulated by giving them a variety of toys, moving their "furniture" around and sometimes hiding their meat. They also add olfactory excitement with spices and perfumes, and when the zoo's reindeer shed, staff scatter some of the fur in the cougars' enclosure. Except when mating or rearing young, wild cougars generally spend a lot of time alone. (African lions are the only big cats that live together in a pride.) But because Miksa, Keira and Tika won't compete for food, mates or territory, they'll remain close companions throughout their lives.

Some big cats in zoos are trained as much as possible to move to commands so keepers can assess their health. This is a big change from the old days when animals were tranquillized to check every little thing. "Each cougar has its own personality. Nashi hated training but Merlin loved it, you'd walk by him and he'd put a paw up or roll over all on his own," Barfoot said of the zoo's two previous cougars, both of which died of old age.

According to Barfoot, cougars are the most difficult big cat to train that she's encountered in her sixteen-year career. "They're funny, smart and intelligent but also headstrong and mischievous. Tigers, lions and leopards like routines and patterns. Cougars like to change things up and do stuff differently every time. That's why you don't see them in many circus acts. On the other hand, captive cougars are the least aggressive of all the big cats."

Female cougars give birth to litters of one to three, or occasionally more, any time of year. To blend in with their surroundings, the tiny cubs have dark spots on their coats and dark rings around their tails that fade over time. They open their eyes, which are blue for the first year, at around two weeks. In the wild, they stay with their mother learning how to hunt and survive until they're about eighteen months to two years old. At zoos, big cats are often removed from their mother soon after birth and hand-raised. "This is really beneficial to animals that will never be in the wild," explained Barfoot. "It allows them to be comfortable around humans and not to hide or feel upset by their presence. It really decreases their stress level and increases their quality of life."

Zookeepers had full contact with Miksa, Keira and Tika until they were a year old. Then the cats were too big and powerful for it to be safe. "The bond between the animals and keepers is very strong," admitted Barfoot. "Some facilities allow full contact with adult big cats but it's Russian roulette. Sooner or later the animal will simply be itself and follow its instincts. No matter how well cared for it is and how strong a bond there is, a cougar is opportunistic. It's hard for the humans to let go of the full contact but the cats don't care. Human life holds more value than an animal's. If someone goes in the cougar habitat and there is an incident, the cat will be put down. We can't put them at risk just for our desire to be with them. There's no such thing as a tame cougar."

Until the three cougars were a year old, zookeepers entered the compound most afternoons to interact with the animals and give a mini-lecture to the public. I had an opportunity to observe one of these sessions during my visit. As 2:30 drew near I could see the cougars getting excited, and when Sasha Puskar and Logan Hendricks approached the door to the habitat the cats rushed over to greet them. Apparently each cougar had formed a close relationship with a particular employee, and Barfoot said they even recognize and respond to regular zoo visitors.

As Puskar began her talk, Keira kept leaping up and chewing her clothes and sucking her hand. Puskar repeatedly pushed the cougar away explaining to onlookers that the cat wasn't hurting her, just playing. "Zookeepers can have two types of relationships with the animals in their care," she said. "They can play a maternal role, which means the cougar respects them, or they can act like a playmate, which leaves them open to injury. The cougars don't realize you're not as strong as they are.

In the beginning, staff at Cougar Mountain Zoo had physical contact with Miksa, Keira and Tika, but by the time the trio were nine months old they were getting too big and strong for it to be safe much longer. When they were a year old, all physical contact with humans was cut off. Here, Sasha Puskar chastises Keira for being too rough. *Photo by Paula Wild*

"So, it's time for me to be mom," she added grabbing Keira by the neck, throwing the cougar to the ground and holding her there for a few moments. When she stood up, she pointed her finger at the cougar and scolded it in a firm voice. As Puskar continued her talk, Keira stared up at her balefully just like my dog looks at me after I discipline him.

While this was going on, Miksa and Tika had melted into the background to watch the proceedings, one crouched behind a rock, the other by a small bush. Their bodies were clearly visible but they were so still and they blended in so well that if you weren't aware they were there, you'd never notice them. Periodically, one would creep out, sneak up behind one of the zookeepers and attempt to jump on their back. That's why there were always two keepers in the compound: one to talk and one to watch. Hendricks and Puskar calmly deflected the leaping cougars with a swing of the arm, but it was clear that soon the cougars would be too large for this casual action to work. Even though the cubs were playing, their activity was obviously leading up to adult stalk and attack behaviour. Being hand-raised and developing strong bonds with humans had not diminished their predatory instincts at all.

"It's fun to roll around on the floor with an adorable ten-pound cub but it isn't so cute or safe when it's an eighty-pound cat," said Barfoot. "Most people who get big cats as pets don't have the knowledge or experience necessary to handle them as they mature."

Cougars end up being kept by humans in a variety of ways. In the old days, if a bounty hunter, rancher or rural resident killed a nursing female cougar, they sometimes captured the young and sold them to zoos or kept them as pets. That's how fourteen-year-old Pansy, twelve-year-old Pearl and eleven-year-old Marion Schnarr ended up with four tiny cougar cubs in January 1934. When their dad, August, a trapper and hand-logger, brought the young cats home to Sonora Island, BC, the girls, who had lost their own mother four years earlier, fed the cougars warm canned milk from pop bottles fitted with baby bottle nipples.

Two of the cubs died by the summer but Leo and Girlie thrived. According to a 1938 article in the *Nashua Telegraph Parade of Youth,* the girls treated the cougars like dogs, teaching them to "jump through the girls' arms, play tug of war, catch food thrown to them, etc., as good as any circus cat." "Teaching them tricks was easy," Pansy is quoted as saying. "We just let them know

Marion, Pansy and Pearl Schnarr raised Girlie and Leo from tiny kittens until the cougars died at ages three and six. The sisters taught the cougars a variety of tricks and kept them in line with slaps to the head. The cougars weren't friendly with strangers, especially men, and often attempted to kill livestock. *Photo mcr015624 courtesy Museum at Campbell River*

who's boss. Anytime we want them to stop doing something we slap them. They quit then."

Leo and Girlie were affectionate and loved to play with the girls but didn't like men—even August. They'd hiss at strangers and on occasion knock a visitor down and sit on the person until one of the girls hauled them off or August bopped them on the head with a piece of wood. After Marion caught Leo stalking the family pig, the cougars were kept chained up unless supervised. Over time, increasingly heavy chains were needed as the cats periodically broke free to roam the island and molest neighbours' livestock. But they always came home, and even though they caused trouble, the girls loved and looked after the cats until they died, at ages three and six.

In 1962 Stan Brock, a good Samaritan to orphaned or injured wildlife, was offered a wild puma cub while on a five-minute airline stopover in southern British Guiana (now the Cooperative Republic of Guyana) in South America. He took the cat home with him to the Dadanawa Ranch located in a remote part of British Guiana. There Leemo, as she was called, joined a menagerie that at times included wild cats, dogs, deer, monkeys and other creatures. Brock didn't tame or train the animals but he named them, fed them, treated their ailments and, in most cases, gave them free run of the ranch house yard.

Born in Britain in 1936, Brock attended private school until his father accepted a job in South America. By age sixteen Brock was working at the large and remote Dadanawa cattle ranch. While there, he became fascinated with wildlife and also appalled at the lack of health care available to people residing in isolated regions. Folks of a certain age may remember Brock as the handsome and daring co-host and associate producer of Mutual of Omaha's popular television show *Wild Kingdom*. He went on to star in two movies, write three books and create his own television series, *Stan Brock's Expedition Danger*. In 1985 he founded the Tennessee-based Remote Area Medical volunteer corps, a non-profit society that provides free health care services to people in the United States and other countries.

But back in the 1960s, Brock was a bush pilot, a research associate for the Royal Ontario Museum Department of Mammalogy and manager of the Dadanawa Ranch. Leemo soon established her place in the hierarchy of wildlife Brock had taken in. She was buddies with an ocelot called Beano but terrorized all the others. Except Chico, the jaguar. In *More About LEEMO,* Brock confessed he worried that Chico would break his chain and there would be a terrible fight to the death. Chico was the heavier and

Powerful legs and long claws make climbing trees second nature to cougars. Here a South American puma called Leemo scampers up a coconut palm. Stan Brock, who cared for Leemo, said she could scale a fifteen-metre (fifty-foot) tree faster than most men could run the same distance on the ground.
Photo courtesy Stan Brock

more aggressive of the two but Brock described Leemo as having the speed and agility of a "lightweight boxer" and wasn't sure who would survive the battle.

Timid around humans when she was young, Leemo became more aggressive as she matured and many of the ranch staff were wary of her. But she was affectionate with Brock and often shared his bed. They wrestled together and she often jumped on his back pretending to bite his throat. "I was never concerned," he said.

Stan Brock, who later starred in the television series *Wild Kingdom* and *Stan Brock's Expedition Danger*, became involved with wildlife when he managed the Dadanawa cattle ranch in South America. He formed a close bond with Leemo, who often shared his bed. *Photo courtesy Stan Brock*

"She never even snarled at me." But Brock was amazed at how easily the puma could knock him down. "She'd run up beside me, wait until one of my feet was at its extreme rear motion and then tap my ankle. It worked every time." (A Texan with a pet cougar said it used the same technique to trip his children.)

Leemo employed this method of bringing down prey when she tackled the ranch's cattle, sheep or horses. Brock once watched her raise a front paw and run on three legs beside a sheep waiting for the perfect moment to strike its ankle. And on several occasions he saw her stalk a flock of quails then rear up as they took flight and bat one into her mouth with a paw. Leemo always chirped and came when Brock called her unless she was in stalking mode. Then, nothing except a vigorously wielded broom or a slap on the head would get her attention. Brock tried to prevent the cat from killing ranch animals but was never angry when she did, as "she was only acting on her instincts."

When Leemo stalked an animal, she placed each hind foot in the exact spot the forepaw had been. And even when circling around, she never took her eyes off her prey. Brock often observed Leemo reacting to moving objects more than a kilometre (up to a mile) away and was convinced that her eyesight was "as good at a distance as a human's and a lot better at short range."

Brock considered Leemo's greatest assets her speed for short distances, her coordination and her strength. "She can catch a deer from a standing start with a twenty-yard handicap, hit top speed within thirty feet and maintain that for well over a hundred yards," he wrote. "Her athletic prowess probably surpasses that of any other feline, regardless of size, including the leopard. She leaps from tree to tree like a monkey grabbing a branch by the forepaws and, as it gives way, leaping to another. It's like watching Tarzan swing through the trees."

When Leemo was four she died while Brock was in Venezuela. "She got into a fight with her friend Beano," he said. "She outweighed him many times over and had him down on the ground and was on top of him. But the ocelot grabbed Leemo by the throat and hung on until she asphyxiated. No one was able to stop them in time."

In addition to providing a home for orphaned animals, some individuals, like David and Lyn Hancock, have obtained cougars for educational purposes. The Hancocks were planning a film series that would encourage people to respect and conserve wildlife in British Columbia. When a cougar hunter shot a female near Campbell River, BC, and planned to use her four kittens as training bait for his hounds, David intervened and took them home. The couple lived in a small bungalow in Vancouver; Lyn taught at a nearby elementary school while David studied zoology at UBC. Their dream was to buy property on Vancouver Island and open a small zoo to promote conservation.

"Private zoos were much more prevalent in 1967," Lyn said. "I knew quite a few people who kept cougars but everyone was supposed to have a scientific or educational permit. Attitudes were different in those days and keeping and displaying wildlife wasn't uncommon. Regulations are much stricter now."

In her book *Love Affair with a Cougar,* Lyn related how the cubs joined the Hancocks' menagerie of dog, fur seal and a variety of local seabirds and raptors. "They were all for research or education or breeding in captivity because populations were dwindling in the wild," she said. Lyn taught a class of high-IQ students and was able to create her own curriculum, so from time to time the cougars and other animals accompanied her to school. Some also appeared on television programs. Eventually Lyn found foster parents for the three female cougars, keeping only Tom at home. Right from the beginning he was the most docile and people-friendly. Lyn later discovered why. He had cataracts and could hardly see.

All the cubs formed strong attachments with their caregivers and Tom, perhaps because of his disability, was especially close to Lyn. There were a few tense moments: when young, the cougars often escaped over the back fence to roam the neighbourhood and they all showed an unhealthy (from a human's point of view) interest in small children. And once on a trip to Little Darcy Island to let the cougars roam free, Tom became extremely jealous of a friend of Lyn's, causing her great concern.

"It's hard to resist a cute cuddlesome fur ball with blue eyes who begs to be fondled," Lyn wrote in her book. "It's almost impossible not to pick it up, let it lick your cheek, jump in your arms, knead and paw. But when that same kitten with its grown-up teeth, sandpaper tongue and towering body pins you to the ground and you yell for him to stop or you turn on the water hose or hit him with a two-by-four, he is going to feel frustrated and never comprehend. You have turned on him, not he on you. He has done the same all his life, so why not now?" Friends who owned cougars told Lyn it was best not to let them jump on or knead humans when they were young as they'd be too rough when they got older. But it was already too late.

After the Hancocks moved to Saanichton on southern Vancouver Island, Tom was boarded at zoos up-island while a suitable enclosure was prepared for him. But Lyn, who'd never had or even liked cats, had fallen in love with the cougar. Every weekend she found a way to visit and spend the day with Tom in his cage. A video a friend made showed Tom's reaction when Lyn gave a chirping whistle from the parking lot. He'd pace and gaze in the direction she'd approach from, obviously excited.

Lyn Hancock developed a very close relationship with Tom, a cougar she cared for since he was a kitten. But as he grew older, he sometimes bit her or forgot to sheath his claws when they were playing. *Photo courtesy Lyn Hancock*

"People freaked out when they saw me in the cage," Lyn recalled. "He'd run and jump, knocking me down, then knead my body with his massive paws and suck on my fingers just like any kitten who has been removed from its mum when young. His tongue was like sandpaper, I had to put bandages on my fingers to protect them." Zoo visitors often thought Lyn was being attacked. She wasn't frightened, however, as she knew Tom was only playing. But she knew it was a dangerous game. "It was teetering on the edge," she said. "As Tom matured and grew larger, he played rougher. Sometimes he forgot to sheath his claws or bit when excited. Even though we both weighed about 150 pounds, I didn't have nearly the strength and agility he did. I was worried a few times.

"People must have a reason to have a cougar, educational, scientific or otherwise," Lyn emphasized. "Because of their strength and underlying predatory instinct they can be a danger to others. You can't ever entirely trust a wild animal—as far as they're concerned, they're doing the right thing, doing what they're meant to do."

Against Lyn's wishes, David took the cougar with him as he toured northern BC communities with their first feature film, *Coast Safari.* In Fort St. James a young native boy ran by the cougar as it was being brought into the community hall. Attracted by the movement and the smell of dried moose blood on the boy's jacket, Tom grabbed the boy's sleeve and wouldn't let go. It took David and his assistant a while to get the boy out of the jacket with Tom hanging on the whole time. No one seemed overly disturbed—two RCMP in the audience didn't even get up and the film proceeded as planned. The boy needed a few stitches but was otherwise unharmed. But worried about the possibility of similar incidents, David had Tom put down that night.

Unfortunately, the life of many captive cougars is not as comfortable as Tom's younger years or what the trio residing at Cougar

Mountain Zoo are experiencing. It's estimated that a thousand or more cougars are privately owned in the eastern United States. Figures are even sketchier in Canada; some say there are probably two hundred or so in Ontario alone. But those are only guesses, as many big cats are kept illegally.

"Things are different now but in the past you could buy a tiger or lion for five hundred to a thousand dollars, but a cougar only cost a hundred and fifty," said Carole Baskin, founder and CEO of Big Cat Rescue. The Tampa, Florida, non-profit society is the largest accredited sanctuary in the world dedicated entirely to the care of abused and abandoned big cats. The Captive Wildlife Safety Act was passed in the United States in 2003, making it illegal to sell big cats, including cougars, across state lines as pets. But many people get around that by obtaining a USDA licence, which means the animal is used in some sort of commercial venture. "Unfortunately, it's still far too easy to buy and sell cougars from one state to another," said Baskin.

People purchase cougars for a variety of reasons. They might want to breed and sell them or add a big cat to their roadside zoo. Or maybe they spot a cub at an auction and decide to "rescue" it. Some people are interested in big cats and become collectors. Others want the prestige of owning an exotic pet. And there are even stories about drug dealers releasing big cats during police raids to distract officers while they escape out the back door.

Websites blatantly advertising "cougars for sale" are no longer common, but those in the know say the internet is still a good source for prospective buyers. Or sometimes it's as simple as responding to a carefully worded ad in a newspaper or magazine. "There are lots of people who breed big cats in their backyards or basements," said Rob Laidlaw, executive director of Zoocheck, a Canadian charity that was established in 1984 to protect wild and captive wildlife. "Breeders often say big cats will only mate if they're healthy and happy but that's not true. I've encountered cougars kept in a Toronto basement with dead cubs in a freezer.

"In the past, you could just drive up to a place, buy a cougar and drive out," he added. "There's more scrutiny and criticism about that sort of thing now so you'd probably have to get to know someone and get them to trust you first. But there are still a tremendous number of people who deal in captive wild animals, often with no questions asked."

Exotic or alternative animal auctions are another source of big cats. Regulations about owning cougars vary from strict to non-existent depending on the province or state. Even if legislation is in place, many people get around it by claiming the animal is part of a roadside zoo and is being used for educational purposes. And sometimes they are. But the reality is that many small zoos are not accredited and all too often animals live in deplorable conditions.

Based in Toronto, Zoocheck inspects public and private zoos across the nation and investigates reports of captive wildlife being abused or kept in unsatisfactory conditions international-ly. "Captive wildlife in Canada is under provincial jurisdiction so the rules differ from province to province when it comes to keeping, breeding or selling cougars," explained Laidlaw. "This means there are no standards in some jurisdictions for animal welfare, management or safety. I recently saw facilities with big cats behind two-metre-high fences. The people working there don't realize that with the right trigger, a mature cat could easily jump the fence and kill someone. Visitors assume they're safe but that's not necessarily true.

"Some provinces do a lot, others do nothing," he added. "For instance, Ontario has no regulations regarding exotic wildlife in zoos, kept as pets or in menageries. A person could go out today and buy a cougar, tiger, spitting cobra and monkey, stick them in cages and put up a zoo sign without any pre-inspection or licensing. In Ontario you need a licence to operate a hot dog stand or nail salon but not a zoo."

Keeping a captive cougar is way different than having an oversized house cat. Cougars require a large enclosure that resembles their natural habitat as much as possible, along with a prepared zoological diet to ensure proper nutrition. And they need regular check-ups by vets specializing in big cats, as well as enough physical and mental exercise to keep them fit and stimulated. This maintenance requires a huge investment of time, commitment and money. Adequate fencing alone could cost seventy thousand dollars or more.

Authorities estimate that the majority of big cats being kept as pets are illegal. If a person wants to be legitimate, they need to research and pay any licensing fees required in their region and possibly purchase insurance as well. In 2008, one Ontario man was forced to pay a $5,500 annual insurance premium to keep the cougar he'd hand-raised since it was a kitten. Apparently finding an insurance company to cover the cat—Lloyd's of London finally agreed to do so—was almost more difficult than raising the money. Another drawback with big cats as pets is that they spray urine to mark their territory. Not only is it messy and stinky, but it's nearly impossible to get rid of the strong ammonia-like smell.

But the biggest problem is that, around age two, the formerly adorable kitten becomes difficult or even impossible to handle. Despite the best of intentions, the reality is that very few people outside of accredited facilities have the resources, knowledge and experience to safely care for a big cat once it matures. A person who purchases a cougar kitten may be able to hold and play with it for up to a year and then have the responsibility and expense of feeding and looking after a pet they can't touch for the next twenty.

The responsibility of securely maintaining a captive big cat is no small matter. There are numerous accounts throughout Canada and the US of "pet" cougars suddenly and seemingly without provocation reaching through cage bars or scaling four-metre (fourteen-foot) fences to attack people. In 2001, a pet cougar in Nevada escaped and hopped aboard a school bus. Luckily, no children were present and the driver exited unharmed, shutting the door behind him. More than one child has been mauled at a birthday party where a cougar was the featured attraction. And even cougars that have been bottle-fed by their owners since they were tiny have caused trouble. In June 2005, an Ohio resident was loading his 90-kilogram (200-pound) cougar into a van to take it to an educational program for Cub Scouts when it attacked him. The same month and year, a New Jersey man suffered severe injuries from his hand-raised cougar. And being declawed and having filed teeth didn't prevent a pet cougar from severely mauling two children in Texas.

"At Big Cat Rescue, we've found that after leopards, cougars are the scariest big cat to handle," said Carole Baskin. "If a cougar sees a child or small volunteer, they instantly and constantly focus on them as easy prey. Nothing you do will divert a cougar's attention once it fixates on someone—you can bang on the cage or spray it with a water hose and it will still remain fixated on what it sees as easy prey."

So far, there is no record of any person being killed by a captive cougar. But there have been some close calls. Doug Terranova, an exotic animal owner and circus trainer based out of Dallas, Texas, had worked with big cats for thirty years when he was attacked. Like most in his profession, he'd experienced dangerous moments. But as Terranova explained in the Animal Planet documentary

Cougars fixate on potential prey—be it wildlife, livestock, a pet or a human—with an incredible focus that is extremely difficult to disrupt. And when it comes to humans, they're particularly attracted to young children and small adults, perhaps because they appear more vulnerable.

Fatal Attractions: The Deadliest Show on Earth, the decision to clean his cougar's cage on his own nearly cost him his life.

It was a cold day so he phoned his employees and said he'd look after the animals himself. When he got to the cougar's cage, Terranova realized he was breaking his rule about no one entering the enclosure on their own. But he'd worked with the cougar for close to fifteen years, so figured it would be okay. Since it was cold, he decided to scatter sawdust on the floor and sweep it up rather than hosing out the cage. Looking down at the floor and bending slightly put him in a vulnerable position. Being alone made him even more so. And when he scooped the sawdust into a large garbage bag, picked it up and turned his back, the cougar's predatory instincts kicked in. It leapt on Terranova, severely mauling him before he could escape.

It's extremely difficult to get rid of a pet cougar after it's outgrown its welcome. Most zoos only accept young orphaned cougars or those that have been born in another zoo. So people sometimes sell their unwanted animals to canned shoots. In these situations an animal is kept in a confined area so it cannot escape and it is then shot. At one time, internet hunting—allowing the "hunter" to shoot the animal with a remote-controlled gun from their computer—was even proposed by some.

Other times, people simply release big cats that are no longer wanted. While it's possible a cougar raised in captivity could survive in the wild, their chances of making it decrease radically if the animal has been declawed and/or defanged. And familiarity with humans, combined with having no hunting experience, means these cats may approach people or otherwise act inappropriately and be shot. Wildlife agencies believe that many cougar sightings in eastern Canada and the eastern US are of cougars that have escaped or been released from captivity. It's not unusual for sightings to spike after legislation is introduced that requires owners to spend money on licences, insurance, cage modifications and/or beefed-up security. Some cougars end their days in big cat sanctuaries but many have been closed due to lack of funding or are already operating at capacity.

All too often, once they mature, pet cougars are banished to a pen in the garage or backyard where they become isolated, bored or worse. Unfortunately, the ultimate fate of many captive cougars is one of abuse and neglect. One cougar cub in Texas was bought under the table for fifty dollars. Her claws had been removed with wire cutters and her paws became infected. And when her baby canine teeth were ripped out, her jaw abscessed. Another cougar, in Nevada, was kept in a chicken coop on a .58-metre (23-inch) chain for six years.

But perhaps the most heartbreaking story belongs to Max. He spent a decade confined in a 3.5 by 3.5 metre (12 by 12 foot) horse stall in a barn in Poetry, Texas. Adjacent stalls contained nine more cougars, nine African lions and one tiger. The only outside light came from two windows high on a wall and the animals were never let out of their pens, never received any mental stimulation or veterinary care, and only had minimal interaction with humans. When their owner died the summer of 2011, people attempting to care for the animals didn't know what to do beyond tossing packages of meat still wrapped in plastic into their pens.

In-Sync Exotics, a Texas-based wildlife rescue and education centre, was called in. When they arrived the big cats were emaciated, dehydrated and sick and their enclosures and water containers looked like they hadn't been cleaned in years. In an empty stall they discovered a shallow grave filled with the bones of previous feline residents. The non-profit society found a new home for Max at Safe Haven Rescue Zoo in Imlay, Nevada, but had no way of getting him there. That's when volunteers from Big Cat Rescue agreed to donate their time and expenses for the nearly 8,850-kilometre (5,500-mile) journey. Until he was loaded in the van for the trip to Nevada and released at Safe Haven, Max hadn't been outside or walked on grass for ten years. Today, staff at the sanctuary say he always bounds out of his den to greet them with a chirp and purrs continuously.

Private ownership of big cats gained international attention in October 2011, when Zanesville, Ohio, resident Terry Thompson

Max spent the first ten years of his life confined to a barn stall with little or no exercise, mental stimulation or veterinary care, and irregular supplies of food and water. When his owner died, volunteers from Big Cat Rescue drove Max to his new home at Safe Haven Rescue Zoo in Imlay, Nevada. There he romps in a large outdoor enclosure and has everything he needs. Lynda Sugasa, executive director of the facility, said, "Despite his horrible past, Max is a very sweet cat and purrs constantly." *Photo courtesy Safe Haven Rescue Zoo*

released his collection of wild animals shortly before committing suicide. Due to public safety concerns officials were forced to shoot and kill nearly fifty animals, including three cougars. Not long afterward, organizations like Big Cat Rescue, the International Fund for Animal Welfare, the Humane Society of the United States and others were lobbying for the passage of the Big Cat and Public Safety Protection Act, which, if passed, would make it illegal to breed or possess big cats as pets in the US. People already owning cougars would be allowed to keep them providing they met certain regulations, and highly qualified, licensed facilities—such as accredited zoos, wildlife sanctuaries and research institutions—would be exempt.

As of mid-2013, Canada had no federal animal act regarding big cats and other animals in zoos or menageries. "Right now in many areas, municipalities have to deal with any problems," said Rob Laidlaw. "As well intentioned as they may be, they don't have the knowledge or expertise required. It's a ridiculous and inconsistent mishmash of rules and regulations from one province to another. Canada's a terrible country when it comes to captive wildlife legislation; they have better regulations in China and India."

Keeping wild animals in captivity is a contentious issue and, in the case of big cats, potentially dangerous to both the animals and humans. The emotional appeal of a small, furry kitten might be hard to resist but the plight of many captive adult big cats is deplorable. us and Canadian governments need to join forces to enact and enforce legislation that will ensure the well-being and secure containment of wildlife in captivity, as well as the safety of any humans they may be near.

CHAPTER 7:
Unexpected Encounters

His whole movement more silent than the drift of the
down that the wind blows from dry fireweed.

—RODERICK HAIG-BROWN, *Panther*

"**Y**ou got a cougar in there," yelled Charles Wuester. It was just after 11:00 p.m. and parking attendant Tim Loewen wasn't sure he'd heard the Blue Bird taxi driver correctly. But when the man repeated himself, Loewen closed the metal security gate of the underground parking lot just in case. Then he jumped in the cab to tour the three-hundred-car parkade. They didn't get far before the headlights revealed an animal. It was March 3, 1992, and there was a cougar at the venerable Empress Hotel. And unlike the tiger whose skin was hanging above the fireplace in the Bengal Lounge upstairs, it was very much alive.

When night manager David Woodward answered Loewen's phone call, he was sure the sighting was a mistake. How could a cougar make its way along busy city streets into downtown Victoria? The Empress Hotel was across the street from the bustling Inner Harbour and kitty-corner to British Columbia's legislative buildings. Woodward decided Loewen must have seen a big yellow dog. But earlier that day the *Times Colonist* had run an article warning residents that a cougar had been spotted at the University of Victoria, Uplands Golf Course and Beacon Hill Park, each sighting a little closer to the heart of the city. To be on the safe side, Woodward had bellboys lock the doors connecting the garage to the hotel.

According to *Cat Attacks: True Stories and Hard Lessons from Cougar Country,* when conservation officer Bob Smirl arrived at the Empress a crowd of two hundred, as well as an assortment of newspaper and television reporters, were gathered outside

Few people see a cougar in the wild, so discovering one at the Fairmont Empress in downtown Victoria, BC, was a huge surprise. Escorting the sedated cat out of the underground parking garage is (from left) Sgt. Gary Green, Victoria Police Department; Frank Wolf, Saanich Fire Department; and Shane Brady, houndsman. *Photo courtesy the Fairmont Empress*

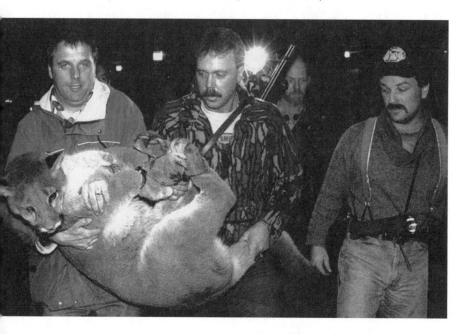

the hotel. Smirl, two dog handlers, their hounds and a police officer entered the parkade sometime after midnight. They were armed with a tranquillizing gun and a .30-30 Winchester. The cougar, no doubt feeling threatened, went for the dogs. It took three tranquillizing darts to knock it out. After a bit of show and tell outside the hotel, the 60-kilogram (132-pound) cougar was taken to a remote area up-island near Duncan. It was approximately four years old, in good physical condition and hadn't acted aggressively toward anyone, so the cat was a prime candidate for relocation.

Even people who work in the woods rarely see a cougar. So it's a shock when one's encountered in an urban setting. But the big cats visit metropolitan and residential areas more often than most people realize. In *Island Gold,* author Dell Hall lists twenty-one cougar sightings and incidences between 1902 and 1989, all occurring within eight kilometres (five miles) of Victoria city boundaries. And several, like the 1926 shooting of a cougar behind the Carnegie Library building on Yates Street and the 1961 killing of another in the doorway of Mac & Mac's hardware store in the 1400 block of Government Street, took place in the downtown core.

George Pedneault lives in Sooke, BC, about a thirty-minute drive from Victoria, and has tracked cougars for sixty years. He believes generations of cougars have followed the same trails into Victoria for as long as the big cats have been on the island. "It's not something we'd recognize as a trail, it's something triggered in their heads," he explained. "A cub won't know to walk along a certain way but somehow it recognizes a path that's been used by other cougars. They won't follow it exactly but they won't be off by more than a hundred feet. And they don't identify it from scent markings—it can be two or more years since another cougar has passed that way but somehow they know."

Pedneault suspects many cougars swim across a narrow section of Finlayson Arm and work their way into Saanich and then downtown. "There's a big rock next to the Uplands Golf Course and if a cougar's in the area, they seem to always go by that rock, I've tracked lots of cats from there." He says others probably travel through the vast green spaces of the Highlands to Sooke and Mechosin, eventually finding their way to Esquimalt, only a short distance from downtown Victoria.

These cats might be surprised to find themselves in such developed human habitat, but it turns out cougars aren't all that unusual in urban areas. An August 2011 article in the *Issaquah Press* revealed details of a study conducted by Brian Kertson as part of his doctoral thesis at Washington State University. Using GPS and radio collars, he documented the travels of more than thirty cougars in the northwestern portion of the state from 2003 to 2008. Among other things, Kertson discovered most of the cats spent seventeen percent of their time in built-up areas. The majority were mature animals who moved through the urban landscape quickly and for brief periods of time. Nonetheless, they were frequently within 500 metres (550 yards) of residential developments, yet rarely noticed.

A telemetry study of eighteen mountain lions near Prescott, Arizona, in 2006 and 2007 revealed that twelve visited urban residential areas. Some did so often while others only made brief forays and left. A number were simply passing through, but some used urban areas as part of their normal habitat. Despite the sometimes frequent proximity of humans, the only time anyone saw or heard about a mountain lion was if one was hit by a car or killed by a hunter. And, at the 10th Mountain Lion Workshop—a forum for research biologists and wildlife managers—held in Bozeman, Montana, in 2011, four presentations focused on cougars living near urban or exurban environments, including Los Angeles.

Dr. Mark Boyce, professor and Alberta Conservation Association Chair in Fisheries and Wildlife at the University of Alberta, where five major cougar studies have taken place from 2004 to 2013, noted, "Cougars adapt fairly well to human presence. They are very secretive. They'll be right in amongst houses in suburban areas and most of the time no one ever sees them." Niki Wilson knows this is true. She was a child in the 1970s when a female cougar with bad teeth bedded down under a neighbour's trailer to have her kittens. The cougar fed on neighbourhood pets and lived in the densely populated Jasper, Alberta, trailer park for weeks before it was discovered.

Unexpected encounters with cougars can happen anywhere, anytime. At the Port of Kalama in Washington state, workers were shocked to see a large cougar at the brightly lit and noisy dock at 1:30 a.m. one night in July 2011. Another middle of the night encounter occurred the same month when RCMP followed a cougar into the town of Sydney, BC, and watched it casually saunter through yards and past businesses on one of the main streets. In December that year, travellers arriving for an early morning BC Ferries sailing had to wait outside the Swartz Bay terminal until a cougar hiding under the administration building was destroyed.

Around noon one day in October 2003 a male cougar was found in the commercial district of Omaha, Nebraska; it wasn't until someone spotted a long tail sticking out of the bushes surrounding the Lewiston, Idaho, Safeway store parking lot at 3:00 p.m. in May 2011 that anyone realized a cougar was there. Two months later a resident of Bonner's Ferry, Idaho, looked up from his dining room table to see a cougar staring at him through the sliding glass door. He said it didn't appear concerned about being in a residential neighbourhood and walked around just like a pet would. A janitor noticed a mountain lion in the courtyard of an office building in

John and Verena Vomastic knew wildlife roamed around their Manitou Springs, Colorado, home during the night but they weren't prepared to see a mountain lion staring through the window in broad daylight. At one point the cat stood up and put its paws on the window and the Vomastics worried it would break the glass. Luckily, the young adult decided it had seen enough and sauntered away. *Photo by Verena Vomastic*

downtown Santa Monica, California, at 6:00 a.m. in May 2012. One morning in August 2012 a cougar tried to enter Harrah's Casino in Reno, Nevada, via the revolving door, and in May 2013 a mountain lion was found hiding in an aqueduct in downtown Santa Cruz, California.

For the most part, cougars make their way into urban areas by way of river drainages, golf courses, parks and greenways. They end up in unusual places for a variety of reasons. To begin with, a burgeoning human population means more subdivisions, many of which are located on formerly vacant property and often abut land that's still in its natural state. No bounty means that in some areas the cougar population is larger than it was fifty years ago. Deep snow can bring cougars into areas where it's easier to hunt. And if there's a shortage of their preferred food source, deer, cougars may go into or near communities to hunt raccoons, squirrels and other small animals. A dog or cat can become an easy meal and one a cougar will look for again. Deer are an attractant too, of course. So if Bambi and cohorts are chowing down on the courthouse lawn, it's entirely possible a cougar will drop by for dinner.

It's the cats that don't make their way out of town or find good hiding places before dawn that are apt to get in trouble. Most normal, healthy cougars avoid humans and are adept at observing without being seen. So if one starts showing itself during the day or acting nonchalant around people in an urban or suburban environment, something is wrong. The cougar may be habituated, old, weak, sick, young or overly curious. The Cougar Network's 2007 *Puma Field Guide* noted that "puma seemingly have become less wary of humans near residential or recreation areas in puma habitat." If a cougar's not afraid of humans, people need to be extremely cautious around it.

Many cougars that appear in inappropriate places are young juveniles. When cougar cubs separate from their mother, usually at around eighteen months to two years of age, they need to become self-sufficient. Like riding a bike, taking down a deer or even a raccoon takes some practice before any real skill is developed. And finding and killing prey is even more difficult for cubs that have been orphaned or abandoned at an earlier age, so some young cougars may come to town looking for a meal that's less strenuous to obtain.

Most adult pumas have a permanent home territory, which can encompass 390 square kilometres (150 square miles) or more. A female with kittens, however, will significantly reduce her range to remain close to her young, yet has the added pressure of finding more prey to feed her family. *Photo courtesy Florida Fish and Wildlife Conservation Commission*

The biggest challenge for young adult cougars is the struggle to find their own territory. Most mature cougars have a permanent home range that may fluctuate with the seasons. Range sizes vary depending on prey density, terrain, habitat and whether a female has kittens of not. According to *Cougar Ecology and Conservation*, edited by Maurice Hornocker and Sharon Negri, males typically have larger ranges than females, which in good conditions can be roughly 195 to 390 square kilometres (75 to 150 square miles) and 65 to 130 square kilometres (25 to 50 square miles) respectively. If prey is scarce or habitat is poor, a male's range may be as large as 1,800 square kilometres (700 square miles) or more. Although

While mature mountain lions may visit or pass through urban areas, it's often young adults that get into trouble. They're still fine-tuning their hunting skills, as well as trying to establish a territory of their own. This is a risky time for the young cats, especially males who are often challenged or even killed by mature males defending their territory.

male territories may overlap to some degree, in most cases they go to great lengths to avoid each other.

According to *Cougar Management Guidelines,* a collaborative effort by thirteen cougar biologists and wildlife managers to synthesize all information about managing cougars available up to 2005, virtually all young adult males disperse about 85 to 100 kilometres (53 to 62 miles), or sometimes further, from their birth area, which may be a way of ensuring genetic diversity. Females, however, are more social. It's estimated that fifty to eighty percent of female offspring either replace a resident female in their home range or establish a territory that partially or fully overlaps with other breeding females. Young males have the most difficulty finding a spot to claim as their own. If they venture into a mature male cougar's territory they will be chased out—or even killed.

Like human teenagers, young adult cougars may be full size, or nearly so, but haven't quite figured out how to make their way in the world. And they don't always display the best judgement when it comes to honing their survival skills. These are the cougars that often find themselves in tough situations. And it isn't always in backyards or city streets. In February of 2011 David Roberts and his wife, Nancy, were enjoying a quiet evening at their Palomar Mountain home northeast of San Diego, California. Then the glass patio door "violently sprung open." When David saw a mountain lion half a metre (two feet) away from him, he jumped up on the couch and started yelling as loud as he could. Nancy, sitting nearby, added her screams to the racket. Looking surprised at the commotion, the cougar ran out the door. The Roberts think it may have been after their cat, which was in the room with them.

Three months later, Jesse Taylor entered his garage to chase away what he thought was a raccoon or other small animal. The Taylor family lived in Herperia just north of San Bernadino, California. But instead of a raccoon, Taylor found himself face to face with a mountain lion. Fish and Wildlife officials tranquilized the animal and released him in the San Bernadino National Forest. The Taylors suspect the lion had been in their garage for three days.

One night in October 2012, a Dexter, Oregon, couple woke up to find a cougar in their bedroom. Apparently it had chased their dog in through the pet door and upstairs into their bedroom. They ran out on the deck and yelled for help but before anyone arrived the cat had gone back out the door.

"In California it's nearly an everyday occurrence to have a mountain lion in a garage or in a residential area," said Marc Kenyon, the black bear, mountain lion and wild pig programs coordinator for the California Department of Fish and Wildlife. "We're noticing that mountain lions occur in and around humans and human development a lot more than previously thought. Studies have tracked them with GPS collars that give a specific location every two hours. The results show them moving in and around human habitat and subdivisions and sleeping in backyards on a routine basis yet causing little concern for public safety. For the most part, this is just the reality of how lions make their living in these areas.

"The take home message here," he added, " is that we've had collared lions in the area for twelve years and during that time only had one type yellow incident, all the rest were green." The California Department of Fish and Wildlife has a colour-coded system of guidelines that regulates how personnel respond to mountain lion sightings. Green indicates the animal is not acting in an unusual or aggressive manner and there is no cause for concern. Yellow means there is the potential for threat; for instance, a mountain lion is seen near a school when children are getting out. And red signifies a physical altercation between a human and a mountain lion. In 2013 a new policy was adopted that gives officials more options for dealing with potential human conflict situations where the mountain lion has not acted in an aggressive manner.

Cougars may enter buildings out of curiosity or because they're looking for a place to hide or find prey. And it doesn't only happen in California. Twenty-four-year-old Denise Mueller was in her bedroom one morning in 1989 when the window of her basement suite in Victoria, BC—approximately 1.5 kilometres (almost one mile) from the Empress Hotel—shattered. A cougar fell through the glass, landing at her feet. Mueller ran into the closet and closed the door. Baying hounds and men barged

Mountain lions frequent urban areas much more frequently than most people imagine. And they enter buildings on occasion. This young adult was photographed in a restroom at the Chatsworth Reservoir in Los Angeles County. *Photo courtesy National Park Service of California*

through the window after the three-year-old cougar, which was shot beside Mueller's bed.

Nine years later, in 1998, Craig Grebicki, a salesman for Scott Plastics, was just about to take a break from making phone calls when he noticed a movement in his peripheral vision. To his amazement he saw a cougar placing its front paws on an interior windowsill. With only a filing cabinet and a potted plant between them, Grebicki held his breath. The cat didn't seem to notice him and dropped back to the floor and went into another office. But when it passed another interior window they made eye contact.

Grebicki shoved his desk chair into the doorway and dashed for the back door. As it closed behind him he heard something heavy hit the other side. At the time, the Scott Plastics office overlooked downtown Victoria's Inner Harbour and was within sight of the Empress Hotel.

One evening in August 2012, Angie Prime was sitting in the living room of her home in Trail, located in the West Kootenay region of BC. Her two pomeranian-chihuahua puppies were curled up on the couch next to her and her eleven-year-old border collie was asleep on a nearby chair. The small, slight woman was thinking about taking the dogs outside when she saw movement out of the corner of her eye. The next thing she knew a cougar was leaping toward her. Prime screamed as she threw her arms and legs up in an effort to defend herself. Roused from her nap, Vicious, the border collie, jumped out of the chair and chased the cougar outside. Prime escaped with a couple of scratches; an old, emaciated cougar was shot nearby the next day.

What has to be the most harrowing account of a cougar entering a building, however, was of an encounter in Kelsey Bay on northern Vancouver Island. Ed McLean, a sixty-two-year-old telephone and telegraph lineman, returned with his dog to the cabin where he was staying late in the afternoon of January 26, 1951. While McLean was splitting wood for the stove he noticed a cougar nearby. He'd seen the cat before and wasn't concerned but made sure his spaniel came inside with him. Around 9:00 p.m. McLean looked out the window and saw the cat standing not far away, watching him intently. Thinking it might be attracted to the light or movement, he turned the gas lantern off.

As soon as the cabin was dark, the cougar burst through the window, locked its jaws on McLean's elbow and knocked him to the floor. McLean managed to get on top of the animal and push

In May 2013, Angie Prime and her eleven-year-old border collie/lab cross travelled to Toronto where Vicious was inducted into the Purina Animal Hall of Fame. The previous summer Vicious had leapt to the rescue when a cougar entered an open sliding glass door and attacked Prime while she sat on her living room couch. *Photo courtesy Purina Animal Hall of Fame*

it toward the table. He didn't have his rifle with him but there was a large knife on the table. By the time McLean reached his destination, his right arm was badly mauled and his strength was ebbing. Using his left hand, he stuck the knife into the cat's throat far enough to sever the jugular vein. When the cat stopped struggling, McLean crawled toward the door, calling his dog from its hiding place under the bed.

But just as they crossed the doorsill, McLean heard the cougar coming after them. He quickly closed the door and, for a few moments, listened to the heavy breathing on the other side. Barefoot and dressed only in his long underwear, McLean stumbled to the rowboat. To survive, he knew he had to reach another cabin almost ten kilometres (six miles) across the bay. A strong wind, loss of blood and drifting in and out of consciousness resulted in the voyage taking two hours. At the cabin McLean tried to call for help but was unable to reach anyone. And he was so cold he couldn't even light a match to start the wood stove. Somehow he managed to cover himself with a sleeping bag before passing out.

The next morning, twelve hours after his ordeal began, McLean made contact with the outside world. When help finally arrived, his blood-soaked underwear had to be cut away from his body. After receiving first aid at the company's office McLean was taken to the hospital in Campbell River, where he was treated for loss of blood, exposure and multiple injuries. In the meantime, Fred Dingwall and Bill French visited the scene of the attack. As they opened the cabin door they saw the cat's bloody body lying on McLean's bed. It was still alive and tried to attack them but they shot it from the doorway. The badly emaciated one-and-a-half-year-old female cougar only weighed 25 kilograms (56 pounds).

Encountering a cougar in a building is extremely rare. But that's not the only unlikely place they've been seen. Due to most cats' aversion to water, many people assume cougars will avoid the wet stuff unless getting a drink or crossing a shallow stream. But it turns out the big cats are exceptionally strong swimmers and don't seem to mind the water at all. In *Island Gold,* Del Hall described a cougar swimming from Vancouver's North Shore to Stanley Park, more than half a kilometre (a third of a mile) away. He also wrote about two separate cougars that travelled between the Gulf Islands in 1928. Starting at Gabriola Island near Nanaimo, each cat swam to Valdes, Galiano, Samuel and then Saturna, killing sheep at every stop.

The most gripping story Hall told, though, took place in 1930 just north of Tofino on the west coast of Vancouver Island. Jacob Arnet was heading back to the Mosquito Harbour mill where he was caretaker when he thought he saw a dog swimming. He turned the motorboat toward it and, as he got close, realized it was a cougar. He quickly reversed direction but the cat was close enough to grab the side of his cedar clinker-built boat. As it began to climb aboard, Arnet pried a boat seat loose and swung it at the animal, knocking it back in the water. The rudder got hit in the process, resulting in the boat going in circles with the cougar trying to climb into the boat and Arnet doing his best to keep it out. When Arnet finally got the rudder under control, he glanced over his shoulder to see the cougar climbing aboard again. And so the battle continued. Arnet eventually escaped but the sides of his boat were badly scratched.

In 2012 alone, several groups of people out on the water witnessed cougars swimming long distances. Two of the cougars were near Sechelt on the Sunshine Coast of BC while a third was a short ways from Tahsis on the west coast of Vancouver Island. In each instance, the cougar turned and swam directly toward the boat.

While there are numerous stories about how far cougars can swim, one is supported by scientific evidence. In *Cat Attacks: True Stories and Hard Lessons from Cougar Country,* authors Jo Deurbrouck and Dean Miller mentioned a UBC wildlife program student who radio tracked a cougar from "the wild heart of the island [Vancouver Island] straight through Nanaimo...When it reached the busy waterfront, the cougar jumped in and swam four miles through the ferry lane to built up Gabriola Island."

So what does it mean to have cougars sauntering through neighbourhoods, strolling city streets, leaping through windows and attempting to board boats? It's a reminder that cougars are

Cougars usually make their their way into urban areas via green spaces such as golf courses and parks and by following river drainages. They don't mind water and have been known to swim long distances.

curious, stealthy, unpredictable and sometimes bold. And that in some regions of Canada and the US, human and cougar territories are overlapping to a greater extent than ever before. More people are living and recreating in cougar habitat and more cougars are visiting and even living and hunting in or near urban areas. Whenever large predators share the landscape with humans the potential for trouble is present. And that means people who live, work or visit cougar country need to know how to respond in the unlikely event they encounter a cougar.

CHAPTER 8:
The Predator

For sheer killing ability, I don't think any cat
in the world surpasses the mountain lion.

—MAURICE HORNOCKER, wildlife biologist,
British Columbia Magazine

In his autobiography, frontiersman and folk hero Daniel Boone recalled seeing a panther "seated upon the back of a large buffalo" with its claws "fastened into the flesh of the animal wherever he could reach it until the blood ran down on all sides. The bison struggled mightily but to no avail." Chances are the bison outweighed the panther by at least 635 kilograms (1,400 pounds) but that didn't prevent the cat from successfully bringing it down.

The cougar is an exquisitely built killing machine. Disproportionally long rear legs provide power for spectacular leaps while overdeveloped front legs ending in huge paws possess superb strength for gripping and slashing prey. Like all cats, cougars are incredibly flexible. As the Florida Fish and Wildlife Conservation Commission explained, "A cat's vertebrae are largely held together by muscles instead of ligaments, allowing it to twist, compress, lengthen and turn in pursuit of prey." An added bonus is that the front legs attach directly to the shoulder blades, letting cats creep up on prey while remaining low to the ground, and loose, baggy skin permits a wide range of motion. Kilo for kilo, a cougar is ninety percent pure muscle. Cougars, especially pregnant females or those feeding young, require a high-protein diet to fuel their muscular bodies. While ungulates graze most of their waking hours, cougars that take down big prey usually follow a feast and fast regime. A cougar that hasn't eaten in a while may gorge on up to five kilograms (ten pounds) or more of meat and blood at one time. When full, the cat drags or carries its catch a short distance away, scrapes out a shallow recess to stash the carcass in and lightly buries it with sticks and leaves to hide it from scavengers. If natural debris isn't available, a cougar will make do; once a deer carcass was discovered in a backyard covered by pieces of lumber. After eating, a cougar will usually take a nap in a secluded spot nearby, then feast again, with the whole process repeating itself over the course of one to several days.

Deer are generally the mainstay of a cougar's diet but they'll eat any form of meat. This includes large game such as elk, moose and bighorn sheep, as well as smaller animals like rabbits, porcupines and mice. Maurice Hornocker once saw a cougar eating grasshoppers. When researchers in Pacific Rim National Park Reserve on the west coast of Vancouver Island analyzed cougar scat and prey carcasses, they found deer and harbour seals tied in second place as dietary sources, followed by river otters, sea lions and mink. The mainstay of the local cougars' diet—up to twenty-eight percent—was raccoons.

In a February 2012 Postmedia News article by Larry Pynn, Danielle Thompson, a resource management and public safety specialist in the Long Beach unit of the park, speculated, "Young cougars lacking the skills to take down deer may be exploiting easier, smaller prey. Some cougars may also defer deer hunting to

Most cougars primarily feed on deer but other mammals such as raccoons, beavers and badgers (pictured here) can also form a substantial part of their diet. And, although they are stalkers, cougars are also opportunistic and will evaluate any potential prey that crosses their path.

the coast's dominant wolf packs." She also pointed out that feeding on marine animals didn't mean cougars were plunging into the ocean to tow sea lions to land; they were most likely picking off young, old, sick or injured animals resting on the beach.

Just like people, cougars also have food preferences. Although the big cats rarely attack cattle, they have a history of doing so in Arizona. And while researching cougars on Vancouver Island, Penny Dewar noticed beavers were a significant food resource for those living near a swampy area. There are also stories about mountain lions in California with a taste for pork and one in Arizona that was particularly fond of porcupine.

A University of Alberta study in the west central portion of the province clearly showed that individual cats had strong preferences for specific prey. And it wasn't always a case of game being abundant or convenient to kill; some cougars actually went out of their way to hunt a particular species. "We found some extreme cases of selectivity," said Professor Mark Boyce. "Big males seemed to really specialize when it came to larger prey. One killed seventeen feral horses, five moose, three elk and two deer. Some would pick off a bighorn sheep and then go get another one; we even had a female cougar that hunted bighorn sheep. They also attacked llamas—people sometimes keep them to guard livestock against predators but that doesn't work with cougars—we tracked one that killed and ate seven llamas."

Cougars that take down large prey generally kill a deer every eight to fourteen days. They may roam 20 kilometres (12.5 miles) or so a day in search of food and often shift their range with the seasons depending on where the deer are. Females with young cubs won't travel as far, and those providing meat for larger off-spring need to hunt more often. But no matter what the age or condition, a cougar's primary goal is to find food.

Due to a relatively small lung capacity, which makes running long distances impossible, cougars are stealth hunters who sneak up on their prey. On beaches, wolves can be seen out in the open, noses in the air or on the ground searching for scent. But a cougar will move through the tall grasses and brush bordering the edge of the sand, slinking behind driftwood and boulders or anything else that provides cover. Harley Shaw, a retired wildlife research biologist who worked for the Arizona Fish and Game Department, noted that the lions he studied seemed to have two basic movements: hunting and travelling. And that aside from closing in on prey or being chased themselves, they seldom moved faster than a walk.

Cougars don't perch in trees or hide at the side of a trail waiting for their next meal to walk by. But if something happens along, chances are they'll check it out. They hunt by stalking and are perfectly content to trail prey for an hour or more, waiting for the perfect opportunity to strike. "It's very unusual for a cougar to stay in one place very long," explained Boyce. "If we had a radio-collared cougar in one spot for three or four hours, it was always on a kill. We got data from the collars every fifteen minutes. There was always a slow, steady stalk followed by a fast dash at the end, never an ambush."

COUGARS THAT ATTACKED HUMANS IN CANADA & THE US 1812–2012

255 cougars total

58% condition unknown   42% known

CONDITION (when known)
42% skinny or starving   48% healthy
6% injured or sick   4% recently eaten

SEX (when known)
51% male   49% female

AGE (when known)
59% young   34% mature (2.5–7 years)
(less than 2.5 years)   7% old (7 or older)

(rounded to nearest percentage)

"A stalking cougar shows no sign of excitement, it is cool, calm and deliberate," wrote Roderick Haig-Brown in *Panther*. "Its instinct is always to follow something, a deer, a racoon, a man...it follows not a scent but a motion." And, like a meditating Zen master, a stalking cougar is intensely focused to the exclusion of everything else. They rarely shift their gaze from their intended victim, even when changing direction or creeping around to another position. In *Out Among the Wolves: Contemporary Writings on the Wolf,* Barry Lopez refers to the visual exchange of signals between predator and prey as "the conversation of death."

Just the thought of being stalked by a big cat stirs a primal fear. Actually experiencing the hard stare is an event that becomes indelibly imprinted on the psyche. "It was a beautiful October afternoon after we'd had a lot of rain," Liz Buckham recalled the spring of 2012. "I wasn't going to walk far, just to the bridge and back." But when the sixty-six-year-old reached her destination, the fine day and mellow jazz playing on her iPod persuaded her to keep going. As Buckham passed the last house on the road and headed up a trail, she realized she'd forgotten her knife and small canister of pepper spray. She'd been carrying them on a regular basis as cougars had been reported in the area. But she'd been concerned about cougars for thirty-eight years and had never seen one. In fact, one of the first things she did when moving to Merville, a rural area on the central east coast of Vancouver Island, in 1974 was buy a knife in case she met a cougar. "That was unusual then," she said. "Everyone thought I was overreacting because I was from Ontario and we didn't have cougars back east."

Partway down the trail, Buckham noticed it had grown up a lot since she'd been there last. "Suddenly I felt anxious and picked up two stout sticks, one for each hand," she said. She could hear someone hammering in the distance and picked up her pace. That's when she noticed the cougar tracks in a partially dried mud puddle. But they were going the same direction as she was so she hoped the cat was well ahead of her. Then the trail ended and she was back on a road with vehicles passing by. Gradually she relaxed enough to throw one stick away. When Buckham decided to head home, she considered going the long way around on the road but was tired, so she opted for the river trail shortcut.

It was around 4:30 p.m. when Buckham strode up the trail embankment to the road, tossing the other stick aside as she did so. *"I'm at the bridge—I'm safe—only ten minutes to home!"* she thought. But just as she was about to step onto the wood planking, a flickering motion caught her eye. She thought it was a dog but as it came around the corner of the bridge railing she saw it was a cougar. "I felt its very focused stare. I couldn't see its eyes because of the lighting but I felt that attention. That extremely focused attention."

Buckham stopped and so did the cougar. Bending over to get a stick or rock seemed too risky so the petite woman shot her arms straight up in the air as high as she could. "There was no discernible reaction and I felt really vulnerable with my torso exposed," she said. "A tingling went up my spine and I thought I was going to faint."

Buckham knew that, no matter what, she couldn't take her eyes off the cougar. "Go on, get out of here," she said, not loudly but firmly the way she'd speak to a dog. The cougar kept its head down, staring intently. With her arms still in the air, Buckham wiggled her fingers, hoping the cougar would think she looked too weird to eat. The cat's ears twitched and she took that as a good sign. She yelled again but the cat didn't respond so she stamped her foot vigorously.

The stare down continued, then the cougar looked briefly to the side. Buckham hoped it was scouting out an escape route. "Then it moved a paw in my direction," she said with a quiver in her voice. "The paw tapped the bridge deck a couple of times before he put it down. He was coming for me! I mustered all my energy and yelled as loud as I could, 'GET OUT OF HERE!'

"I could see its underbelly flopping as it made two leaps and disappeared across the road up a driveway," Buckham said. "That's when I realized how big it was. It never made a sound; it was totally silent even when bounding away."

Buckham didn't dare cross the bridge to go home so she ran the other way until she found someone to give her a ride. At the bridge they saw a woman and a small child out for a stroll so the

Liz Buckham had just tossed the branch she was holding aside when a cougar appeared on the other side of the bridge and began to approach her. *Photo by Paula Wild*

driver gave them a lift too. As soon as Buckham got home she called the neighbour to tell them a cougar had run down their driveway. They went out to investigate and saw the big cat darting away from the chicken coop.

It's impossible to know if the cougar had been stalking Buckham but by not hiding or running away, it was most likely exhibiting predatory behaviour. And considering the proximity and the cat's ability to leap thirteen metres (forty-five feet) in one bound, she was in grave danger. Even though Buckham was not physically injured, for over a year she was afraid to go for a walk or bike ride by herself. Time has dulled the intense fear but she still feels uneasy when she's at the bridge or bent over in her garden.

Since cougars are sprinters, not marathon runners, they steal up on their quarry, say to within six to fifteen metres (twenty to fifty feet) or so, and then make a short, fast dash—at up to seventy-two kilometres (forty-five miles) per hour—to leap onto their victim's back. If possible, they like to attack from a higher elevation; sometimes the impact alone is enough to incapacitate the victim or break its neck. Cougars kill by biting the back of the neck to sever the spine, biting the throat to crush the trachea and suffocate their prey, or by reaching forward with a front paw to grab the animal's nose and pull the head sideways or backward until the neck breaks. Jerry MacDermott, a wildlife technician with British Columbia's Ministry of Forests, Lands and Natural Resource Operations, once tracked a cougar in the snow that had ridden an elk's back down a steep incline for about 90 to 140 metres (100 to 150 yards) until it eventually broke its neck.

A December 2001 video taken in New Mexico and posted on the Cougar Network's website shows an approximately 70-kilogram (150-pound) cougar tackling a 120-kilogram (265-pound) mule deer. When the video started the cougar was hanging by its front paws onto the side of the running buck and slowly pulling itself on top of the trophy animal. Once astride the deer, the cougar bit the buck's neck in an attempt to break it. But as the narrator pointed out, the buck was in rut and hormonal changes had caused its neck to thicken. As the buck stopped running, the cougar flopped to the ground, hanging from the deer's lower neck trying to suffocate it.

The deer kicked the cougar's head and body repeatedly with its sharp hooves but the cougar never flinched. Using its powerful forelegs and claws, the cougar pulled the deer's head, then its entire body, to the ground. The buck thrashed and kicked mightily but the cougar held on. Eventually, seeming to realize it needed to change tactics, the cougar released its hold on the neck and clamped onto the deer's snout, crushing it with its powerful jaws. There is no doubt the cougar suffered serious injuries during the struggle, but from the initial leap to the final scene it only took five minutes for it to asphyxiate its prey.

Wild canines primarily rely on scent to find and track their prey, so they have long muzzles and small eyes. Cougars depend on sight more than smell and have large eye sockets. In *The American Lion* author Kevin Hansen discussed the special membrane behind a cougar's retina, which reflects light and provides extraordinary

Cougars have large eye sockets as they rely on sight more than smell. Their short, muscular jaws are built to open wide and their incredibly strong canine teeth can exert tremendous force. Based on the small size and the teeth, which are small and not worn or yellowed, this skull probably belonged to a juvenile cougar eighteen months to two years old. *Photo by Paula Wild*

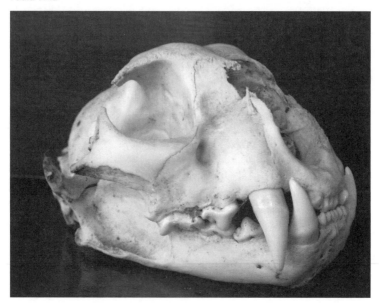

vision day and night. It's estimated a cougar can see in the dark six times better than a human.

Cougars have relatively small heads with short, powerful jaws built to open wide and long canine teeth—up to five centimetres (two inches) on adults—made for tightly grasping and killing large prey. These very strong canine teeth have punctured and crushed the skulls of wolves, horses and humans and are resistant to bending even under extreme force. The smaller front teeth are used to pluck hair and fur from an animal before it's eaten, while the blade-like teeth in the rear are for ripping meat from a carcass and cutting through tendons and sinew.

A cougar has four claws on its rear paws and five, counting the dew claw, on the front. These incredibly sharp tools are used to catch and hold prey. Unlike those of bears or canines, cougars' claws are normally retracted except when they are scratching trees or during an attack. In one news article, Brian Keating of the Calgary Zoo and the University of Calgary referred to a cougar's claws as "razor blade steak knives."

Once its prey is dead, a cougar slices open the skin and removes and buries the stomach and intestines. The cat then enters the body from below the ribs and feeds first on the high protein, vitamin-rich liver, heart and lungs. There is no chewing involved, the cat simply rips the meat into strips and swallows chunks whole. Unless it is chased off a kill by other predators or hunters, a cougar normally consumes up to seventy-five percent of a carcass by weight.

Cougars aren't lazy but they are prudent about their energy expenditure. They're always looking for an easy meal, even if they've recently eaten. Female ungulates that are pregnant or have just given birth are vulnerable, as are newborn fawns. Bucks in heat, with their one-track minds, also fall into this category. Animals that are young, old, sick or injured are at increased risk, especially if they are separated from the herd, or look like they easily can be. This method of selecting prey also applies to livestock and pets, and humans if they hike alone, lag behind or bend over to tie a shoe.

It was a typical misty morning at the Marble River estuary located north of the town of Port Alice on northern Vancouver Island. At the top of the slope a couple of ravens cawed from a stand of old-growth Douglas fir. Jack Scott had planted trees up the logged off clear-cut and was now working his way down the hill. It was February 1991 and he was moving quickly, both to keep warm and to make money as a piece-worker. Around 8:30 a.m. he paused to watch the noisy birds. "They were flying in circles, one would land on a lower branch and then the other would do it. They repeated this over and over," he said. "I'm really interested in birds and thought maybe this was some kind of courtship ritual. So I kept looking back at them every few minutes."

When one of the ravens flew straight at the thirty-nine-year-old, he ducked quickly to avoid being hit. "The raven went back to the tree line squawking really loudly," Scott said. "I couldn't figure out what they were up to." He continued planting, working alongside a downed cedar snag that was too big to climb over. Then the hair on his head bristled. Scott planted the tree he was holding and looked over his shoulder but didn't see anything. As he planted another tree he had a strong feeling he was being watched so he straightened up and turned around.

"The only reason I noticed it," he said, "is because it blinked. It was a big cougar—maybe 130 to 140 pounds—crouched about 60 to 75 feet away, staring at me intently. In a fraction of a second it was bounding towards me. My first instinct was to throw my shovel at it but I knew if I didn't brace myself for the impact, I'd be a goner. So I ran forward and hit the cougar in the chest with the point of the shovel."

When Jack Scott was attacked by a cougar he used his treeplanting shovel to deflect the cat's initial lunge. He's shown here at the cut block near the Marble River estuary on Vancouver Island where the attack occurred, holding the shovel that saved his life. *Photo by Jean-François Hautcoeur*

Treeplanting shovels have narrow, elongated blades that make them easy to use in the bush. Scott figures the spear-like weapon was the only thing that prevented the big cat from becoming airborne. He shouted but none of the nearby crew heard him. "I startled the cougar when I hit it," Scott explained, "but it never let up. I began working my way towards the landing, yelling and throwing sticks and rocks at its face and hitting it with the shovel. But every time I turned, it tried to get on my back."

Scott had changed tree bags that morning and accidently left his emergency whistle in his pack down on the logging road. That's where he was headed but it wasn't easy with eighteen kilograms (forty pounds) of trees on his back. The ground was pockmarked with big holes full of rainwater. He fell into several, bruising his legs and soaking his tree bag, making it even heavier. Finally he was able to shrug the bag off. "Then the cat moved in closer and ran beside me," he said. "I managed to get my Stanfield's off and threw it quite a ways in front of the cougar. Having something with my scent on it seemed to confuse it."

With the cougar distracted by his shirt, Scott ran. Reaching his pack, he grabbed his whistle and blew on it continuously as loud and hard as he could. "The cougar came right down to the road and lay down just like a regular cat," he said. "Its ears were back flat against its head and it was whapping its great big tail—it looked four or five inches thick at the base—on the ground. Then someone else showed up and it went into the bush.

"The cougar never made a sound the whole time it was after me," Scott added. "If I would have thrown my shovel at it I wouldn't be here now. As for the ravens, I think they were alerting the cougar to my presence so they'd have something to scavenge." Ravens do scavenge cougar kills and in *The Tiger,* author John Vaillant mentioned carrion crows that followed tigers on a regular basis.

Cougars often watch and study their prey as they assess the risk-benefit ratio of launching an attack. Once the big cat has selected its victim, it rarely shifts its gaze from them even when creeping around into another position.

Twenty-one years later, Scott continues to work in the bush but he is a lot more cautious. "I still go out by myself but I always take a knife and whistle," he said. "I was arrogant when I was young but you know that saying, 'Once you step off the road in a remote area, you become part of the food chain'? It's true, the rules are different out there and most people aren't fully aware of that."

Cougars rarely attack humans, but why wouldn't they? They are carnivores, and people are meat—and with no built in defence mechanisms such as sharp teeth, horns or hooves, pretty defenceless prey at that. Yet the risk of being attacked by a cougar is low to extremely low. Of course, if you live, work or recreate in cougar country, the odds of encountering the big cat and being attacked increase. In the last two hundred years in Canada and the US, cougars have attacked 281 humans resulting in 55 fatalities. That works out to an average of .28 people killed by cougars per year. (Actual figures are probably higher as few records were kept in the early days and some suspected deaths could not be confirmed as caused by cougars.) By comparison, 34,767 people were killed in motor vehicle accidents in the United States in 2012. That's an average of 95 per day.

But cougar attacks are increasing. In the last hundred years (1912 to 2012) 201 attacks occurred, with 124 of those—sixty-two percent—taking place since 1990. Granted, early attacks sometimes weren't recorded. But according to the data available, there was a minor spike in the 1950s (12 attacks compared to 5 the previous decade), perhaps due to some states and provinces ending or phasing out bounty hunting. There was a sharp rise in the 1970s and 1980s with 19 and 25 attacks each decade. And then a huge jump in the 1990s with 62 attacks, and another 58 taking place between 2001 and the end of 2012.

Cougars attack people for many reasons, with each cat, person and set of circumstances creating a unique situation. The cougar might be young, old, sick or starving. A high density of cougars in an area or a low prey population can cause aggression as males compete for territory and all cougars compete for food. Cougars will also act aggressively if they feel their prey carcass is threatened and females will respond the same way if they have cubs. Cougars that prey on livestock or pets may become accustomed to the human environment and begin to view people as another form of prey, and the quick movements of a jogger, mountain biker or child may trigger the cat's chase/kill instinct. Cougars continually run off their kills by wolves may seek other sources of nutrition.

Because attacks on humans are so unusual, there is speculation that some cougars experience chemical changes in the brain, due to nutritional, genetic or other conditions, that affect their behaviour.

Necropsies on some cougars that attacked humans revealed diseases such as rabies and feline leukemia.

Some believe logging affects cougar behaviour, too. "Deer do really well in old-growth forests where there is a healthy understory," explained Danielle Thompson, a wildlife biologist with Pacific Rim National Park. "They also do well in recently logged areas where there is lots of lush, new growth. It's during the in-between stage when tightly spaced trees grow back and choke out the undergrowth that they don't do well. That's when deer are forced out of their habitat and concentrate in marginal habitat near and in human use areas where they can find food. And despite their natural wariness, cougars will follow.

"Changes to the landscape such as extensive logging roads and more trails also has an impact on wildlife and alters their behaviour," she added. "It's energetically costly for an animal to move through a dense understory. So they travel on the same roads, trails and beaches that people do, creating an overlap of time and space that increases the chances of an encounter."

One question often debated is whether cougars possess an innate fear of humans or if it is learned. From reading many accounts, it appears that cougars were more wary of humans in the past. In fact, they were commonly considered cowards who only attacked people if they were sick, injured or defending their cubs. In his 1917 book *The Panther and the Wolf,* Colonel Henry W. Shoemaker noted: "The woods [of Pennsylvania] teemed with them... Almost every backwoods kitchen had a Panther coverlet on the lounge by the stove. Panther tracks could be seen crossing and re-crossing all the fields, yet children on their way to school were never molested."

But a lot has changed since the early days of the twentieth century. In the 1970s people began moving out of urban areas and onto rural or semi-rural properties. Some wanted to "get back to the land," plant big gardens and raise chickens, horses or a cow or two. Others were looking for a quiet neighbourhood complete with star-studded skies and a nice view. An acre or more, often with dense vegetation and adjacent to similar properties or land in its natural state, provided privacy and more opportunities to see wildlife. The next decade brought an increased emphasis on the benefits of physical fitness, and the manufacturing of lighter-weight, better-functioning mountain bikes in the 1990s meant more people were hiking and biking in rural and wilderness areas than ever before. Also, improved transportation infrastructure meant many city dwellers were only a short drive away from national parks and other wild places. Cougar hunter George Pedneault noticed a change on Vancouver Island when pickups and campers became commonplace. "Around the 1970s, the island really opened up with logging roads into rural areas," he said. "People had to walk in before, but now they can drive in and park their camper or travel trailer next to a nice lake."

Some, like Dave Eyer, don't think cougar attacks on humans are escalating just because there are more people in the woods. Eyer has a degree in biology and has worked as a naturalist, hunting guide and trapper. In his twenties his work in the adult education field took him to the Arctic, where he spent time with Inuit hunters observing the prey–predator interactions between caribou and wolves and between seals and polar bears. That experience, plus bear awareness and safety books by Stephen Herrero and Gary Shelton, reinforced his interest in large carnivores.

Since 1985, Eyer and his family have lived on 65 hectares (160 acres) an hour's drive northwest of Clinton, BC, where seeing wildlife is as common as sitting down to dinner each evening. As owner-operator of Eyer Training Services, he's taught a variety of safety and outdoor education courses. In 2000, he added a bear and cougar encounter program for industry and government field workers, which is now a required course for many employees. He offers a similar workshop for people who spend recreational time in the woods or who live in rural areas.

"The more people in the bush theory would result in more accidental encounters, which could lead to more attacks," Eyre said. "That may be true for bears as the majority of grizzly bear attacks are defensive. But most cougar attacks are predatory. The majority of people are attacked from behind, they're not accidently bumping into a cougar. In BC between 1983 and 2005, thirty-four percent of cougar attacks occurred in developed areas where normal human activity regularly occurs, so cougars are approaching places where people are."

By developed areas Eyer is referring to houses, schools, playgrounds, logging camps, commercial campgrounds and youth camps. His statistics for cougar attacks on humans in British Columbia from the early 1800s to 2005 indicate that ninety-three percent of the attacks were either predatory or possibly predatory. He suspects that cougar and deer biology and genetics play a role in why cougars attack humans. Plus the fact that people now treat cougars differently than they did previously.

"I believe the unrestricted shooting, trapping and poisoning of cougars during the late nineteenth and early twentieth centuries seriously suppressed the cougar population," Eyer said. "Many cougars were eliminated and the survivors took great care to avoid people. That's probably why there were so few cougar attacks on humans before the 1950s.

"There were most likely always some cougars that would attack humans if given the opportunity," he continued. "But up until the 1960s, most hunters, guide outfitters, ranchers, pioneers and government workers carried firearms in the bush. Cougars were thought of as vermin and shot on sight. There are many stories of cougars approaching people but no contact being made. That's because the rifle was handy, loaded and quickly used. The cougar was either killed or ran away and learned not to hang around humans. There's been a cultural shift in how people respond to cougars. Few people carry firearms anymore and a significant proportion of urban people who hike are naively unaware about the dangers of large predators."

Bear expert Gary Shelton echoes those sentiments in his three books: *The Bear Encounter Survival Guide, Bear Attacks: The Deadly Truth* and *Bear Attacks II: Myth & Reality.* "In the early part of the 20th century, people lived off the land," he wrote in *The Bear Encounter Survival Guide.* "They raised food and kept livestock. In those days people didn't tolerate carnivores close by. They couldn't or their crops and livestock would be destroyed. Then in the '70s and early '80s that culture changed. It became easier to grow food in large scale operations and ship it to outlying areas. So people were no longer competing with nature for their food and carnivores weren't such a problem. That meant less bears and cougars were shot and over time their populations have increased."

The majority of attacks on humans are by young cougars, but that isn't always the case. And they aren't always sick or starving either. There are accounts of two- to three-year-old healthy cougars, some that had recently eaten, attacking people. These animals fall within the borderline age of young adults that were perhaps still figuring out how to survive. But mature cougars in good condition also attack humans.

On May 16, 1988, the badly mauled body of a nine-year-old boy was found in the Catface Range just north of Tofino on the west coast of Vancouver Island. Two days later a four-year-old,

Cougars prefer treed, brushy areas or broken ground so they can stalk their prey, sometimes for hours. Many people don't even realize a cougar is nearby until it attacks them.

healthy male cougar was shot in the area. Examination of both bodies confirmed the cougar killed the boy. Thirty-year-old Frances Frost was killed around 1:00 p.m. while cross-country skiing in Banff National Park in Alberta on January 2, 2001. There was evidence that the healthy, eight-year-old male cougar found standing over her body had stalked her for some distance. One year later, a healthy three- to four-year-old male cougar that had recently eaten attacked sixty-one-year-old David Parker a short distance from his home in Port Alice, BC.

Frances Frost was moving faster than a walk, which may have triggered the cougar's chase/kill instinct. David Parker had ducked under an overhang to shelter from a rain squall so he might have appeared vulnerable. No one knows what the young boy was doing but he was a small human. The one thing they all have in common is that they were alone when they were attacked or killed by a fit, mature male cougar.

In a paper presented at the 3rd Mountain Lion Workshop, held in Arizona in 1988, Dr. E. Lee Fitzhugh stated that "Mountain lions are large, strong predators and can treat people as prey." His theory proposed that cougars learn to view humans as prey by watching another cougar attack a human, by seeing a human after a botched deer kill and attacking the person instead, or by having their kill instinct triggered by seeing a person exhibit prey behaviour such as moving quickly.

In "Managing with Potential for Lion Attacks Against Humans," the wildlife biologist speculated that cougars may encounter an unknown species on numerous occasions before deciding it is prey. He noted that felines are programmed to attack anything that moves quickly away from them and mentioned personal knowledge of cougars following people from a distance while they were on foot or horseback and considered this type of behaviour a possible form of habituation.

"We understand through ecology that some predators engage in prey switching, moving from their primary prey, such as deer, to an alternative such as horses or sheep," explained Marc Kenyon of the California Department of Fish and Wildlife. "Not every lion, but some may consider people as potential prey. It depends on a lot of things: their nutritional needs at the time, their hunting experience, the availability of traditional prey. I believe every lion that attacks and feeds on a person has made the decision that humans are a potential prey item."

CHAPTER 9:
Keeping Safe in Cougar Country

What's amazing is not that cougars attack people
but that it doesn't happen more often.

—DAVE EYER, Eyer Training Services

Clarence Hall saw the cougar lying at the base of a spruce tree twelve metres (forty feet) away. It appeared to be sleeping. Confident it hadn't noticed him, he quickly headed back to his truck. He was about eighteen metres (sixty feet) from the vehicle when it felt like a baseball bat struck him hard on the left side of his neck.

"There was no noise, I never heard it coming," he said. "But within a split second I was pulled onto my back and felt a warm trickle of blood filling my left ear. The cougar's canine teeth were fully embedded as it shook my head the way it would to kill prey."

A bricklayer by trade, Hall had been tracking cougars for more than thirty years and was on contract with the Ministry of Environment to hunt problem predators. That winter, ten cougars had been shot in the Bella Coola Valley on British Columbia's central coast. So Hall wasn't surprised when a conservation officer called to say a cougar had killed a dog on the Nuxalk reserve. Hall arranged for his grandson-in-law to come by to pick up six of his redbone and black and tan hounds and headed to the reserve to scout out the situation.

It was close to 10:00 a.m. on January 24, 2000, when he arrived at the residence of Cecilia Mack and her adult son, Barry. Barry showed Hall where the cougar had killed his dog. It was below freezing with a skim of fresh snow on the ground so while Barry went inside to put on some warmer clothes, Hall considered his options. The cougar had been shot at eight hours previously and the dog's body had been brought inside, so he figured the cat was long gone. Also, he wasn't sure about the protocol of carrying a rifle on the reserve and so left his .30-06 in the truck. "That was my first mistake," Hall admitted. "The second was turning my back on the cougar."

Now, the seventy-four-year-old was flat on his back with two of the cougar's canines in his scalp, one in the side of his neck and the other piercing his throat five centimetres (two inches) from his jugular vein.

Hall recalled a day long ago when a dog trainer told him that if he was ever attacked by a dog to place his hands behind its bottom canine teeth to seize control of the jaw. Without hesitating he put the thumb, forefinger and middle finger of his right hand into the cougar's mouth. "Very easily I pushed downwards on the lower jaw releasing the teeth from my neck and pushed upwards releasing the upper canines as well," he said. Worried that the cougar would rip his belly open with its claws, which were draped over his torso, Hall placed his left arm over the cougar's front legs and squeezed them against his chest as hard as he could.

He'd started yelling for help as soon as the cougar attacked but didn't know if anyone could hear him. And although he'd gained control of the cat's jaw, his hand was being mangled. "I decided to take my hand out of the cougar's mouth, throw my right arm over its neck, then push its pug nose into the snow as hard as I could until it quit breathing," he said. "But as soon as I removed my hand, the cougar started chewing on the top of my head. I knew this was a life and death struggle and only one of us was going to survive."

As Barry came back outside he heard Hall shouting and saw man and beast locked in a bloody embrace. The twenty-year-old dashed into the house for his rifle. When Hall noticed Barry with his small .22 Hornet, he called, "Come closer, closer," afraid he'd be hit by a bullet as he wrestled with the cougar. Barry was only thirty centimetres (a foot) away when he pulled the trigger four times.

"I didn't hear the shots, I just felt the cougar jerk and become still," Hall said. He had to pry the cougar's teeth from his skull before he could stand up. After steadying himself for a moment he walked to the house with Barry. "I was going to drive myself to the hospital but had lost my keys in the struggle," he said. "Then Chris King pulled up and gave me a ride."

Although Hall nearly lost his right hand and underwent three hours of surgery, during which he received more than a hundred stitches, he bears few physical scars from his ordeal. There's a mark where one of the cat's teeth punctured his skull and part of a vein in his left arm is permanently collapsed due to the force of his grip on the cougar's legs.

Hall attributes his survival to keeping a cool head and knowing what to do. And despite his age and slight build, he was wiry and strong, whereas the six-year-old cougar only weighed thirty-six kilograms (eighty pounds), about two-thirds the normal weight for a cat that age. Also, even though it's not unusual for cougars to eat porcupines, the female's gums, paws, forelegs and chest were loaded with quills. Hall knew if the cougar had been healthy or a large male, he might not have made it. Either way, he wouldn't be alive if Barry hadn't shown up with his rifle.

Clarence Hall, shown here with his wife and hounds, had been tracking cougars for thirty years when he was attacked by one in 2000. He used a tip from a dog trainer to prevent the cougar from killing him until help arrived. *Photo by Rick James*

It's extremely unusual to see a cougar and even more so to be attacked by one. People are much more likely to be injured or killed in a motor vehicle accident, yet most Canadians and Americans are around cars every day. Collisions are avoided by paying attention to what's going on and using tools such as seatbelts, child safety restraints and airbags in case an accident does occur. Most people employ these precautions without even thinking about them. And that same common sense should be present whenever a person is in cougar country.

The first step is to be aware of the environment. Abnormally noisy birds or an abrupt silence—like one woman noticed just before a cougar grabbed her small dog—can indicate the presence of predators. Likewise, a gathering of ravens, jays, crows or eagles may mean they're scavenging a nearby cougar prey carcass. No matter where a person is, the outdoors has its own community of creatures. For them, survival means knowing who's in the neighbourhood and what they're up to. If a person is observant, they can pick up clues from wildlife and birds' behaviour. And it's easier to tune in to what type of song the birds are singing—or not—if you aren't looking at a mobile device or using headphones.

Just as it's prudent to look both ways before crossing a street, people in rural and wilderness areas should be aware of the signs of animal life around them. But humans seldom see cougars. Their coats blend in with most landscapes and they're masters of silence and stealth, adept at seeing without being seen. In *Animal Dialogues,* author Craig Childs mentioned a thirty-six-kilogram (eighty-pound) mountain lion that walked through the Arizona desert making less sound than Childs' fingers did running through the sand. Jessie Dickson and a friend were hiking in Alum State Park in California and were within a metre and a half (five feet) of a mountain lion before they noticed it. The only reason they saw the cat was because it turned its head to watch them.

It's not unusual for radio-collared cougars in California to be tracked crossing golf courses, entering backyards or watching people as they walk on trails. "If you spend any time in the woods, I can almost guarantee that you've been close to a lion and not known it," said Walter Boyce, wildlife veterinarian and professor at University of California, Davis. What people are most likely to see is the orange, red or green eyeshine of a big cat in the dark or the tip of its long cylindrical tail as it leaps across a trail or road.

Although secretive and discreet, cougars do leave physical signs of their presence if a person knows what to look for. Cat tracks are wider than those of canines and the four toes are closer to the

A large male cougar's paw may be ten centimetres (four inches) long and nearly as wide. The cat's toes are closer to the pad than a canine's and the pad has three distinct lobes at the rear. Bear and canine paw prints usually show marks from their nails; cougars normally travel with their claws retracted so claw marks are seldom seen. *Photo courtesy Florida Fish and Wildlife Conservation Commission*

pad, which has three distinct lobes in the rear. A table in *Cougar: Ecology and Conservation* indicates an adult male's paw may be as long as ten centimetres (four inches) and nearly as wide. Because their claws are retractable, they are rarely seen in tracks.

A walk in the woods might also reveal drag marks where a cougar has moved its prey or a pile of leaves and debris where it has cached a carcass. Cougars bury their scat, which is usually segmented with rounded ends, so it is seldom noticed. But males will scrape up dirt and leaves then urinate or defecate on them. These piles serve as territorial markers warning other males to stay away. A female in heat may urinate on such piles to signal her availability. Cougars also rake their claws on trees and logs as a way of communicating amongst themselves. Creating these scrape piles and scratch marks is similar to a person posting a "No Trespassing" sign on a fence or signing in on an online dating website.

Odours can also provide an indication about what's going on outdoors. The scent of spoiling meat may signal a cougar's prey cache, and the big cats have their own peculiar smell. Craig Childs mentioned a strong scent like "sex, fur and sweat." In "A Mountain Lion Visits," Carmen Lucas described "a very strong, yet strange odor" she noticed while outside in southern California. And despite four decades of working in the bush, tracks in the snow and a "rank, catch in the back of the throat smell that bypassed logic and said danger right down the spine" convinced Harold Macy to leave his Vancouver Island woodlot and head home for the day. Which brings up a good point: whether you're walking down a dark alley late at night or strolling through the woods, pay attention to your intuition. If you hear or see something suspicious, or just get a funny feeling, leave the area.

And this care and attention isn't only required in remote areas. Many people think cougars only attack humans in the wild back-country, but nearly half of all human-cougar altercations take place near urban centres, often along trails and rivers, as well as in campgrounds and parks. In "Cougar Attacks in British Columbia: Early 1800s–2006," Dave Eyer noted the top locations for attacks were in the bush, on a trail and at or near a house, followed by beaches, lakes, rivers and creeks. People who live in rural or wilderness regions need to consider the possibility of a wildlife encounter at all times, even if they're just taking a quick walk with the dog or relaxing in the backyard.

The *Bear & Cougar Encounters Course Handbook* used by Eyer Training Services recommends employing four layers of protection: avoidance, awareness, behaviour and deterrents. Avoidance means knowing if cougars are in the area and if there have been any recent sightings, encounters or attacks. If you see a cougar and it doesn't notice you, that's a sighting. If you're both aware of each other, that's an encounter, and an attack is any direct physical contact between a human and cougar or a human using a handheld implement such as a shovel or an axe at very close quarters to prevent contact.

If an attack has recently occurred and the cougar is still at large, the sensible plan is to avoid that location for a while. All parks in cougar habitat should have entrance signs advising, "Cougars frequent this area" or, as needed, "Cougar seen recently." That lets people know they need to be more aware of sounds, sights and smells and to be extra vigilant when moving through forested, brushy trails or while visiting beaches and cleared spots adjacent to wooded areas—in other words, any environment that gives a cougar an opportunity to stalk and come close without being seen.

A key element of rural and wilderness safety is recognizing the difference between defensive and predatory behaviour and knowing how to respond appropriately. A defensive cougar might bare its teeth, growl or swat a paw at you. This is typical behaviour if a cougar feels threatened because its kittens are nearby, or its prey carcass is, or it is cornered with no avenue of escape. Stalking, following and circling with few or no signs of stress is predatory behaviour. A predatory cougar will be intently focused as it gauges the potential cost-benefit ratio of making an attack. As a general rule, if a cougar is agitated, a person should remain

Cougar kittens are born with a pattern of camouflaging spots which slowly fade away over the course of two years or so. The majority of cougar attacks are predatory but a female with cubs—no matter what their age or size—will defend them fiercely if she feels they're threatened. *Photo courtesy Florida Fish and Wildlife Conservation Commission*

calm; if a cougar is calm, a person needs to immediately respond very aggressively.

Because cougars can move so quickly, Eyer recommends preparing your defence, then assessing the situation. If you catch a glimpse of a cougar as it runs away (non-aggressive behaviour), you can count yourself lucky to have seen one of these elusive creatures. But it's also important to remain alert in case it circles around to stalk you. If a cougar exhibits defensive behaviour the appropriate response is to raise your arms in the air, speak calmly but firmly and slowly back away, being careful not to trip and fall and keeping to open ground as much as possible. These actions tell the cougar you are human and not a threat. Don't aggravate the cat by lingering to watch it or take photos. And no matter what, never turn your back on a cougar, even if it appears not to see you. Make eye contact immediately and don't break it; if you're wearing sunglasses, remove them. Staring at an animal is a powerful form of aggression that informs it you are the dominant one. It's also important to remember that eye contact between people and bears is totally different than eye contact between people and cougars. Most bear attacks are defensive and eye contact should be avoided; the majority of cougar attacks are predatory and eye contact is vital.

Like all cats, cougars are curious. Frank Hovenden worked in the bush as a forestry engineer for thirty years, yet only saw a cougar once. "I was pulling a chain [measuring device] uphill and happened to glance behind me," he said. "There was a cougar batting at the end of the chain just like a house cat with a piece of yarn. We looked at each other for maybe twenty seconds then the cougar melted away into the bush... totally silent and invisible in seconds."

A curious cougar can quickly turn into a dangerous one if it learns not to fear people or if a sudden movement triggers its chase and attack instinct. There are records of cougars following people for long distances and watching them for lengthy periods of time. Some evidence suggests they've observed household routines and determined when dogs will be left in easily accessed pens at night. Other times, tracks have indicated a cougar has anticipated a person's movements—or perhaps learned from previous observation—and taken a shortcut through the woods to intercept them farther along a trail. There is speculation that cougars observe humans as a way of determining if they are prey or not. So a cougar that doesn't immediately leave the area when it sees people should be considered dangerous.

If a cougar is watching or following you, that's the time to stand your ground and prepare to defend yourself. "If a cougar exhibits predatory behaviour, a person must immediately act very aggressively," said Dave Eyer. "They need to make a lot of noise, throw things and stand up if they're not already doing so. This lets the cougar know it's lost the element of surprise. It's important to do this at the very beginning of an encounter. Cougars can move very quickly and if a person waits it might be too late to avert an attack."

If two or more people are present they should stay close together to create a united front. Small children should be picked up and told not to cry or shriek as high-pitched sounds may be interpreted as a sign of prey in distress. Older children, short adults or people who might appear vulnerable should move behind the others. Everyone should put their arms over their heads to make themselves appear as large as possible. Waving a hat or jacket overhead also creates a sense of height. "This is the time to dominate the cougar with your voice, body language and actions," explained Eyer in his two-day training course. "The cougar may be deciding whether it can kill someone and you want to convince it otherwise before it comes any closer. If a cougar is very close or even watching from a distance that is a dangerous sign."

Everyone needs to act together to send the cougar a "don't mess with us" message. They must convince the cat that an attack will require a significant outlay of energy and will result in serious injury to itself or possibly even death. No matter what, do not let the cat sense any fear. It is extremely important to project an image of dominance and confidence. Yell, stomp the ground and kick dirt or snow at the cougar. Aggressive tactics like these have convinced cougars to leave the area. Sometimes acting like an animal works too. While hunting with Buffalo Jones one time in the early 1900s, Zane Grey had to keep two cougars treed by himself. Every time they looked like they might jump down, he barked like a dog; in his words, he "bayed at them for an hour."

More recently, twelve-year-old Colton Reeb headed to the outhouse around 6:30 p.m. on August 1, 2007. His family was camping with friends near Clinton, BC. When forty-five-year-old Marc Paterson heard the boy squeal he ran over and found a cougar mauling him. A former construction worker, Paterson kicked the cat as hard as he could with his heavy boots, but the cougar didn't react so Paterson started choking it. The cougar released Reeb and Paterson's dog joined the melee as the man and cat rolled around on the ground. When the cougar squirmed free, Paterson leapt to his feet. The cougar was about a metre (three feet) away, ears pinned to its head and eyes locked on him. Paterson raised his arms in the air and growled "like a grizzly bear." The cougar left and was later shot by conservation officers at the site of the attack.

Throwing rocks and sticks is a good defence but bending to pick them up puts you in a vulnerable position. People have been attacked while crouching or squatting to tie a shoelace, look in a tidal pool or relieve themselves. In groups, only one person, preferably the tallest, should pick up items at a time. If possible, they should step behind others while doing so and grab several rocks or sticks to pass to others. This needs to be done quickly and with as much aggression as possible. Speak in a language cougars understand: bare your teeth, growl and act like you're getting ready to spring into an attack. And don't break eye contact. Cougars often close in when someone glances away—even for a second.

Cougars are stealthy and incredibly focused.

A cougar pauses to drink from a stream (previous page, top); and an adult marks its territory by clawing a log (previous page, bottom).

Cougars have formidable canine teeth (top) and blend into the environment so well a person could walk right by one and never see it (bottom).

It's a common misconception that cougars don't care for water. A GPS collar on one cougar documented a 6.5-kilometer (4-mile) swim. *Photo (top) by Richard Badger*

Cougars, particularly young ones, sometimes appear in unexpected places (next page).

"Ol Dan" and his pup, Sam, bayed this young adult cougar in Waterton Lakes National Park, Alberta, while working on the Castle/ Carbondale Cougar Study. The risky situation resulted in the dogs being leashed and the cougar left alone. *Photo by Brent Sinclair, Porcupine Creek Outfitters Ltd.*

Female cougars with young kittens move them often to decrease the chance of other predators finding and killing them.

Cougar cubs are curious and playful just like domestic kittens.

This cougar (top) was photographed while stalking visitors in Waterton National Park. *Photo by Valérie Domaine*

Cougar kittens may look cute and cuddly (right) but even at three weeks old (left), possess long sharp claws. *Photo (left) by Eric York, courtesy UC Davis Wildlife Health Center*

A female cougar and her young cubs (next page).

A cougar watches the photographer from a tree (next spread). *Photo by Adrian Dorst*

A rare photograph of a cougar catching a fish (previous page, top). *Photo by Tom Ulrich*

Cougars typically eat the heart and liver of large prey first (previous page, bottom).

Cougars have been observed jumping 5.5 metres (18 feet) straight up from a standstill and 18.5 metres (60 feet) down from a tree. They can also run up to 72 kilometres (45 miles) per hour for short distances. *Bottom photo courtesy Florida Fish and Wildlife Conservation Commission*

If you spend any time in the woods, chances are a cougar has seen you while you've been totally oblivious of its presence.

Air horns, whistles and bear spray are good cougar deterrents. And since cougars are masters at sneaking up close and then moving in quickly, all defense gear should be worn on holsters or lanyards outside outer clothing, not carried in backpacks or tucked under jackets. *Photo by Paula Wild*

Predators observe potential prey's body language and actions to determine if they are vulnerable or will be a formidable foe. Any sign of weakness, such as limping or lagging behind, will attract their attention. In *Soul Among Lions,* Harley Shaw wrote about a time in his Arizona research when he inadvertently separated a female cougar and her cubs. He took the three kittens back to Spider Ranch and kept checking the capture sight in hopes the mother would return. When she did, he tranquillized her and took her to the ranch so he could release the family together. As the female began to wake up, Shaw placed the kittens in her cage. But the cat's wobbly, doped-up movements triggered their instincts and the kittens attacked her. Shaw rescued the mom and when he reunited the family the next day, the kittens showed no sign of aggression.

Noise can be a very effective deterrent. If a cougar is exhibiting predatory behaviour, everyone needs to yell as loudly as possible and to use air horns or whistles if they have them. In "Lessening the Impact of a Puma Attack on a Human," a paper presented at the 7th Mountain Lion Workshop in May 2003 by Lee Fitzhugh, it was noted that the duration and intensity of noise is just as important as volume.

One day in the fall of 1999, Bob Evans was enjoying a pleasant afternoon in the woods. He was bent over, intent on filling his bucket with the chanterelle mushrooms found in that particular area of Quadra Island, BC. Then the sixty-nine-year-old noticed a motion out of the corner of his eye. He stood up, looked over a log and saw a cougar running away. *"Great!"* he thought. *"I saw a cougar and it was going the other way."* Then his border collie began barking furiously. "I turned around and staring at me from between the roots of an overturned stump was a bigger cougar," he said. "Because it was so large, especially the head, I thought it was a male and wondered if I'd interrupted something between him and a female."

As the cougar leapt down from the stump and approached him, Evans picked up a three-metre (ten-foot) branch. He slowly backed away swinging the stick with his dog barking by his side. The cougar advanced steadily, remaining just beyond reach of his weapon. "I started to feel panicky and hoped I didn't trip," Evans said. "Then I remembered hearing voices in the distance. The floater jacket I was wearing had come with a whistle so I grabbed it and blew as loud and long as I could, hoping someone would recognize it as a distress signal." Nobody showed up but the cougar left.

"Loud, continuous noise does have an effect on mountain lions," says Marc Kenyon of the California Department of Fish and Wildlife. "It tells them to back off." Kenyon studied the big cats while attending the Universities of Montana and California and has extensive personal experience with the predators. "Every negative stimulus can be broken down into intensity and duration," he explained. "If it's high intensity but short duration, chances are a cougar will think, 'I can live with that.' It's like if one of your neighbours plays loud music every once in a while, you can probably live with it. But if someone jabs you with a pin continuously, you're not going to put up with it. That high intensity and long duration stimulates you to react.

"If someone fires a few shots in the ground, that's high intensity but not long enough duration," he continued. "It will probably startle the cougar and make it pay more attention to the person. But if someone fires multiple shots—say ten shells in rapid succession—that's high intensity and long duration and usually exceeds a lion's comfort zone. Air horns are real loud and can last a long time."

But there are a couple of instances in which noise can attract a cougar rather than repel it. One is the high-pitched voices of children and the other is a hunter using some sort of call to lure game. On a hunting excursion with his son Travis, Dave Eyer took along a deer call and tried the buck grunting sound. After each of the three calls, Travis heard a sound like a stick breaking behind them but no buck appeared. When they hiked out they saw the paw prints of a cougar and realized it had responded to the call.

Another way to deter a mountain lion is to aggressively run toward it, being careful to remain out of reach. "In some instances charging a mountain lion has convinced it to leave the area," Kenyon said. "One night around 10:00 p.m., I was patrolling a campground and noticed a mountain lion lying down cleaning itself next to a tent filled with giggling twelve-year-old girls. I was six feet away with a flashlight but it didn't assess me as a threat and ignored me. So I ran towards it screaming."

The lion ran off but stopped after four and a half metres (fifteen feet) to look back at Kenyon. He shot it with a rubber slug from his shotgun and chased it some more. "Mountain lions don't like an animal or person to be higher than they are," he said. "They attack by jumping on their prey's back so maybe they think, 'Hey, this thing could jump down and try to kill me. This could be energetically costly so I'll just leave.' As I chased the lion, every chance I got, I jumped up on some rocks so I was higher than it. The lion would take off a short ways and get up on a log or something so it was higher than me. We played this game for about twenty minutes, until I didn't feel comfortable being so far away from the camp."

There is one situation where being higher is not an advantage. Cougars kill horses and some even develop a preference for the meat. But in the *Bear & Cougar Encounters Course Handbook,* Eyer pointed out that "unlike bears, cougars usually see the horse and rider as two very different creatures." As of 2013, there were five documented cases of cougars attacking horseback riders in BC. In each case they were after the person, not the horse. If a rider is knocked or dragged off their horse by a cougar, one person should dismount and approach the cat with bear spray while the other riders remain mounted and prevent the horses from bolting. Using bear spray while mounted isn't a good idea as it's too easy for the horse to be affected as much as, or instead of, the cougar.

If a cougar doesn't leave or comes closer after someone attempts to dominate it, it's time to employ your weapons: ideally bear spray or a firearm. A cougar can cover twenty metres (sixty-five feet) in one second so, if you wait to see what it's going to do, it may be too late. Bear spray comes in containers of different sizes that vary as to spray duration (four to nine seconds), reach (5.5 to 12 metres/18 to 40 feet), strength and cost. Eyer says each canister should last six seconds and spray a minimum of 7.6 metres (25 feet). Make sure the spray meets recommended government guidelines and is not out of date. It's also a good idea to practise outside with inert spray or partially empty containers to get a feel for how they work. Flipping the safety latch on and off several times makes it easier to operate, too.

When using bear spray, the cougar must be close enough to be sprayed in the face. Short blasts, repeated as necessary, are better than emptying the can all at once. It's easy, especially for an inexperienced person, to use too much spray too soon. Carrying two cans, or one for each person, ensures there is a backup. If you are downwind from the cougar try to shift your position so you don't spray into the wind and end up inhaling the pepper concoction. If that isn't possible, take a deep breath and close your eyes just before spraying then move quickly to the side. As the spray is released it makes a loud hissing noise, which may serve as a deterrent on its own. Always wear the canister on a belt outside all of your clothing as there likely won't be time to retrieve it from a backpack or even from under a jacket. Anyone using a firearm must, of course, be trained in its use, have the appropriate licences and permits and be in a place where it is safe to shoot without the possibility of injuring others.

Knives save lives. According to Eyer, a person in cougar habitat should carry a fixed-blade knife that is 12.5 to 15 centimetres (5 to 6 inches) in length and has a rubber (or some other type of high friction) grip. The blade should be thick so it won't snap if it hits bone. And it should always be sharp. Spend time trying out knives for heft, weight and grasp. A guard between the blade and the grip will prevent your fingers from possibly sliding down and being cut, and a hole in the grip for a wrist lanyard means less chance of losing the knife if it's dropped or knocked out of your hand. The knife should be carried in a sheath on a belt, outside of all your clothing, and on the side of your stronger arm. This makes it easy to draw without taking your eyes off a predator. It also means you can probably still reach and use the knife if you're knocked down and a cougar is on your back. Bear spray should be worn on your other hip and be positioned so you can draw it with your thumb on the release. A knife should always be your last line of defence when all other efforts to deter a cougar have failed. The primary goal is to stop the cougar before it gets close.

If a cougar runs or leaps at you, try to avoid the impact and remain on your feet. If physical contact is made, guard your head and neck with one arm while battling the cougar with the other. As Eyer said numerous times during his course, "Never play dead and never give up!" Do whatever you can to inflict pain and injury. If you don't have any weapons and a cougar is on you, kick, bite and scratch. Shove a stick in its mouth, ear or nose or bash it with a rock. Focus your efforts on the front of its face, especially the eyes.

And that's just what water quality specialist Susanne Groves did around noon on December 13, 1994. The twenty-five-year-old was standing in the Grass River in southwestern Colorado when she heard rustling on the bank above her. When she saw the mountain lion she thought it was merely curious and would soon leave. But the cat followed her into the shallow water. Groves yelled and splashed water at it but the big cat kept coming. When she slipped it grabbed her by the head and held her underwater. Groves broke free and made it as far as the bank before falling again. She grappled with the lion, managed to get on top of it and shoved her arm down its throat, pinning it to the ground. Then she pulled her forceps out of her fishing jacket and stabbed the lion in the eye. The cat ran off. Groves survived her injuries and an old, underweight female cougar with badly worn teeth was later shot nearby.

In late April 1998 Andy Peterson had spent the day on one of his favourite hiking paths at Carpenter Peak in Colorado. The twenty-four-year-old was on his way back to his vehicle when he saw a mountain lion under a ponderosa pine. Peterson didn't think it had noticed him so he quietly began backing down the trail. To be on the safe side, he got his Swiss Army knife out of his fanny pack. But the knife made a snapping sound when he opened the blade, causing the lion to turn and stare at him. As a park ranger, Peterson knew what to do: he yelled, waved his arms and made himself look big. The lion charged but Peterson was able to avoid impact. But on the second charge, the lion knocked him three metres (ten feet) into the bushes. A river of blood ran down his face as the lion chewed on his skull. Peterson stabbed the cat but the knife didn't penetrate its tough hide. Then Peterson realized there was a soft spot under his thumb. He plunged his thumb into the lion's right eye. The cat made a loud noise and disappeared. Peterson rarely hikes anymore, and never alone. He also quit working as a park ranger.

It's very important to make every possible effort to deter a cougar as soon as possible. In "Factors Governing Risk of Cougar Attacks on Humans," mountain lion researchers Dave Mattson, Kenneth Logan and Linda Sweanor noted that once a cougar is within one to five metres (three to sixteen feet), odds are it's made up its mind to attack. A chart in *Cougar Management Guidelines* described crouching, tail twitching, intense staring, flattened ears and body low to the ground as pre-attack behaviours with high human risk. Each escalation between encounter and attack requires more vigorous intervention. And once a cougar has tackled its prey, it is loath to let go.

Being with others greatly reduces the odds of a fatality, although it won't prevent an attack. Out of the 281 people attacked in Canada and the US, where it was known if they were with others or not, 87 (thirty-one percent) were alone and 129 (forty-six percent) were part of a group. And that's not surprising, if you look at it

A cougar uses its long tail to keep its balance on quick turns while chasing this snowshoe rabbit.

from a cougar's point of view. Cougars regularly attack deer. The cat picks its victim, stalks and chases it down, and then makes the kill while the rest of the herd runs away. Many people who have been attacked by cougars while in a group or who have gone to the rescue of others say the cougar looked *surprised* when someone intervened or the victim fought back.

"People need to respond very aggressively and immediately in this situation," explained Eyer. "Victims have been saved by others running at the cougar, screaming or yelling at it, blowing a whistle, or waving an oar. If you run away or are paralyzed by fear, it is likely the victim, especially a child, will die. Ninety-nine percent of people who die from cougar attacks are alone. If you stay and fight, the probability is very high that the attack will end, the victim will live and you will not be seriously injured."

Cougars become intensely fixated on their chosen victims. When a woman was attacked at a logging camp near Beaver Harbour on northern Vancouver Island in 1953, her husband rescued her and took her home as she wasn't seriously injured. But when the woman and her husband left the house later, the cat attacked her again. Despite the presence of her husband and other people nearby, the cougar had waited for the woman to reappear.

Unlike bears, cougars seldom attack those who come to the rescue of someone else. In May 1985, Johnny Wilson was camping with his mother and aunt in Pacific Rim National Park. When a cougar attacked the boy, the women chased it off by yelling loudly. But the twelve-year-old was badly wounded and had blood spurting from an artery. The women attempted to stop the bleeding as the cougar circled around them for more than an hour, sometimes with its head less than thirty centimetres (a foot) from theirs. The women carried Wilson to the tent and the cougar ignored his aunt as she ran the five kilometres (three miles) to Pachena Point Lighthouse for help.

No matter what, a person that has been attacked should never be left alone while others go for help. In early August 1985, Lila Lifely heard a little girl scream. Lifely, a counsellor at YM/YWCA Camp Thunderbird, located near Sooke on southern Vancouver Island, was in charge of a few girls on a hike away from the camp. When she investigated the sound she found a cougar holding ten-year-old Alyson Parker by the head as it dragged her into the bushes. Lifely charged the cougar with a chunk of wood, screaming for all she was worth. The cougar initially backed off then went for Parker again. Lifely hit it and this time the cat disappeared into the bushes. The nineteen-year-old was on her

Impressed by the stories a friend of the family told, George Pedneault started tracking cougars when he was in his early teens. Lizzie, shown here, is a special type of Airedale terrier bred to hunt large game. Although not as good at cold calling, this breed is considered exceptionally fearless and brave. Pedneault commissioned the carving he's standing next to after being moved by the beauty of light on a cougar's face as it climbed a tree in Rivers Inlet. *Photo by Rick James*

way to get the first aid kit when she heard Parker moan. Looking back she saw the cougar standing over the girl. Lifely charged and hit the cougar a second time and it vanished into the forest. Not willing to leave Parker again, Lifely climbed a tree to yell for help. But even when others arrived, the cat continued to try to sneak up on the girl.

Parker was taken by vehicle to the nearest hospital and George Pedneault was called in with his tracking hounds. "That was a confusing one," he recalled. Every time the cougar hunter let his hounds loose they wanted to go back down the road. Pedneault thought they were trailing the track backward and kept bringing them back to the attack site. But on the second day, he heard about reports to the RCMP of a cougar looking into car windows on Highway 14. "That crazy cat followed the girl even after she was in a vehicle; he was still looking for her," said Pedneault. He shot the fat and healthy eighteen-month- to two-year-old male cougar a short time later.

Anyone living, working or recreating in cougar country runs a slight risk of being attacked, but certain factors increase the possibility. Being alone may make a person appear more vulnerable and it also boosts the odds of dying from an attack by as much as fifty percent. And cougars often, but not always, attack the smallest person. "They are always assessing the situation," explained Marc Kenyon. "Are you disabled or moving slowly? Are you off by yourself or walking slower because you have a sprained ankle? All of these indicate vulnerability and make you look like easy prey. Mountain lions have evolved by trying to figure out which animal is going to peel off from the group to become an easy target."

Six-year-old Dante Swallow was the smallest kid at his day camp near Missoula, Montana. He was also at the end of a long line of hikers and had fallen behind. When camp counsellor

Aaron Hall heard a commotion behind him on July 31, 1998, he turned to see a mountain lion pulling the boy into the bushes by his head. The story in the book *Cat Attacks* doesn't mention if Hall received training for this type situation, but the authors noted that, despite not having a weapon, the sixteen-year-old had attitude. Hall charged the mountain lion, kicking dirt in its face and booting it repeatedly in the ribs. When the cat released Swallow, Hall straddled the boy the way the lion had—in effect claiming the prey as his own—and stared at the animal fiercely. The lion rushed in, swiped at Hall and reached down to grab Swallow. That's when Hall delivered a hard kick to its muzzle. The cat retreated about three metres (ten feet) and looked back. Hall charged it again and the lion left.

Even when hiking with others, people often step off the trail—alone—to relieve themselves. If you're in high-risk cougar country a sensible solution is to have someone discreetly stand guard nearby. "Most people, especially women, squat to relieve themselves in or on the edge of the forest looking at the beach," noted Shannon Bailey, who, along with her husband, owns property in Nuchatlitz Provincial Park on the BC coast and operates Sea Watch Cabins. "Squatting is a very vulnerable position. I tell visitors they should squat at the edge of the water on the beach and look at the tree line, not the other way around."

Besides being alone or apart from a group, exhibiting prey behaviour by moving quickly or erratically increases the odds of an attack. In "Factors Governing Risk of Cougar Attacks on Humans" the authors noted that the level of activity doesn't have to be intense to increase the risk, and that those engaged in some sort of active movement at the time of attack were twenty-eight percent more likely to die from a cougar attack than those who were more sedentary.

People who enjoy being active outdoors can minimize their risk by going on outings with others, being aware and being prepared. A bike can be held overhead to make a person appear larger or even used as a weapon or shield. And some joggers and mountain bikers wear masks with eyes on the back of their heads hoping to confuse cougars. This tactic has proved successful in the Ganges Delta in India where Bengal tigers kill many people each year. A 1988–89 experiment found that although tigers followed mangrove workers wearing masks, they didn't attack them. In three years, no one wearing a mask was killed. But twenty-nine people who weren't wearing masks died from tiger attacks within an eighteen-month period.

Cougars are active at all times of the day and night but are most active at night and during the hour or so just before and after dawn and dusk. A chart put together by the Mountain Lion Foundation shows cougar activity levels over a twenty-four-hour time period in southern Utah. At forty-three percent, dawn had the highest level of activity, with dusk a close second at forty-two percent. So in cougar country, it makes sense to avoid outdoor activities—especially those that make you look like prey—at night and around dawn and dusk.

Located on the west coast of Vancouver Island, Pacific Rim National Park Reserve includes three geographically separated units: Long Beach, the Broken Group Islands and the West Coast Trail. Sandy beaches, rocky bluffs, the open Pacific, whales and forested trails make the area a hiker's and boater's paradise. And some of the park, such as Long Beach, is readily accessible to even the most casual hiker. People travel from all over the world to experience this magical chunk of BC's west coast. But cougars frequent the area and sightings and encounters within and near the park have increased in recent years.

Signs like this one in the Grand Canyon National Park alert visitors that mountain lions frequent the area. *Photo by Ian Hall*

In an effort to protect both people and predators in the area, staff devote a lot of time to public education and outreach. "The bottom line is wildlife evokes an emotional response from people that affects how they respond," said Danielle Thompson, a resource management and public safety specialist at the Long Beach Unit of Pacific Rim National Park Reserve. "Some people don't do anything, some forget everything they've been told and some follow a bear with their camera. Others have extreme fears about wildlife and don't want to see any. What's really important is for people to condition wildlife to avoid humans by yelling and acting aggressive. If people know the proper way to respond, it's safer for them and the big cats.

"You can never eliminate the risk," she added. "But people can go for their walk or jog later in the morning, earlier in the evening or with a partner. And they can be aware of their surroundings. Having small children in a beach area bordered by dense vegetation or forest is not ideal; it would be better to go somewhere where there are more people and less cover for carnivores to hide. The same goes for camping: if you pick a remote spot, chances are greater that you will see wildlife. And trekking the trails during the shoulder season when less people are around also increases the chance of an encounter." And even though a study showed cougars tend to avoid paths that eighteen people or more use a day, many people have been attacked while hiking popular, well-used trails. It's always wise to be aware and prepared.

A lot of people don't believe cougars pose a threat to humans or discount the possibility that it could happen to them. But personal experience has a way of changing minds. Twenty-eight-year-old Lynda Walters was jogging in Four Mile Canyon west of Boulder, Colorado, when she noticed a mountain lion. It was June 2, 1990, and there had been complaints about lions killing pets in the area. Walters was thrilled to see a lion up close. Until its penetrating gaze made her uneasy. She stretched her arms up over her head and yelled. The lion crouched, flicked its tail and began to creep toward her.

Walters was alarmed as other wildlife had always run away from her. She threw rocks at the cat then caught a flash of movement and saw a second lion sneaking up behind her. She scrambled up a bank throwing rocks and sticks as she went. At the top she quickly climbed a ponderosa pine. Partway up she felt one of the lions scratch her leg as it came up after her. Instantly Walters recalled information from a martial arts course she'd taken. The instructor had stressed how much strength women have in their legs and encouraged them to abandon their inhibitions and be prepared to hurt their opponent. Walters stomped on the lion's head, sending it to the ground. She climbed higher and felt the tree shake as the other lion began to climb the tree. Walters broke off a branch and jabbed it at the lion, yelling as she did so. After she repeated this manoeuvre twice, the lion left the tree.

It was 6:00 p.m. and although she could hear people in the distance, no one heard Walters's cries for help. One of the cats tried climbing the tree again but she banged her stick and it backed down. She was terrified that both lions would come up and kill her as soon as it got dark. Then they all heard a slight noise across the gulch. It was a deer. The lions took off after it and Walters descended the tree and ran home. In his postscript to *Beast in the Garden,* David Baron noted that Walters was so disturbed by the incident that she moved to an area with wide open spaces where it was unlikely a mountain lion could sneak up on her.

Walters isn't the first person to climb a tree to escape a predator. The trick is knowing what to do if it comes up after you. Using bear spray or hitting the animal in the nose with a sharp stick is a good line of defence. Other options include throwing whatever is in your pockets or backpack at it. Kicking a predator while in a tree should be a last resort. "Kick with your heel on the nose and quickly withdraw the foot," Dave Eyer said. "A person must be lightning fast because a predator can bite and hold onto the foot, pulling them out of the tree. This can happen if the person is slow to withdraw their foot or if through their body language they let the cougar know this is what they are about to do. As always, bear spray is best. It causes pain and tells the predator the cost of this attack has just gone way up."

Encountering more than one cougar is not that unusual. It's often a case of young adults travelling with their mother or hunting together for a while after they've separated from her. In such situations, Eyer advises placing your back against a tree or bluff to prevent an attack from the rear and using bear spray or a gun. If you are using bear spray, wait until the cougars are about 3 to 3.5 metres (10 to 12 feet) away and then spray in bursts. If the cougars are on opposite sides of you, you'll have to spray in more than one direction. Chances are, a nose or eyeful of spray will persuade them to leave.

Each cougar has its own personality and each situation has its own dynamics. Unfortunately, there's no guarantee that following any guidelines to avoid or survive a cougar attack means a person will be successful. In each case, a person needs to use their knowledge of animal behaviour and their personal judgement and experience to assess the circumstances. Women have chased cougars off with brooms, umbrellas and tea towels; in other cases it has taken several men with axes to end an attack. What's important is to use whatever resources are at hand and never give up. If what you're doing doesn't work, try something else.

It was just past noon on May 6, 2006, when a pine cone rolled down the hill and hit Hugh Faust's shoe. The twenty-two-year-old university student was birding in Medicine Bowl National Forest in Wyoming. Then two red squirrels burst into loud chattering just up the trail. A few minutes later Faust saw the mountain lion. It was crouched low and staring at him from nine metres (thirty feet) away. The summer of 2004 Faust had worked in South Africa tracking, tranquillizing and studying big cats and other large mammals so he knew what to do. He whipped off his shirt and waved it, yelled and charged toward the lion. It ran to meet him and as they made contact, Faust bashed it in the head with his binoculars. By yelling and throwing sticks and rocks, he managed to keep the cat about a metre and a half (five feet) away. Whenever something hit the lion, it either closed it eyes briefly or looked at the object as it bounced off. Then it refocused its gaze on Faust. And each time he stopped yelling or waving his arms, the stare became more intent, and the cat tensed its muscles and its tail began to twitch.

Faust decided to move out of the aspen and conifer forest cover by crossing a gully into some sagebrush. He knew he'd have to break eye contact to cross the stream so before jumping he gathered some rocks. As he leapt, Faust threw a rock, hitting the lion in the head. But when he landed and looked back, he saw the lion in mid-pounce. He hit it in the head with another rock. As he worked his way further into the open country the lion dropped back. But every time Faust turned away or averted his eyes, it moved in quickly. When Faust reached his SUV the lion disappeared. Faust had used his best defence—his brains—to survive. He kept his wits about him, didn't panic and fought his way to open ground and his vehicle.

Faust figures the encounter lasted ten minutes. "I kept eye contact throughout the whole ordeal, and feel I never scared the cat at all, but did stop it from making the final pounce," he said. "I honestly thought it was going to pounce any second and believe it would have if I had even flinched on the initial rush, or ever presented an opportunity. I've tracked leopards, spotted hyenas, cheetahs, African lions, and African wild dogs on foot in South Africa and have never seen any animal this intent and persistent."

The majority of attacks are unprovoked. Eighty percent of the time, people aren't even aware of the cat before it attacks. And even if they do glimpse some movement, they rarely have time to take any defensive action. Fifty percent of victims need help to fight off a cougar.

In his awareness and defence courses, Dave Eyer advises enjoying the outdoors in a safe manner by employing the colour code of awareness. This method is often used by the military and police and is valuable whether a person is driving on the highway, hiking in the woods or walking a busy city street. Being in white means a person is lost in thought or engaged in conversation or an electronic device to such a degree that they have no awareness of their surroundings. When a person is in yellow they're interested and observant. They may be working or talking but frequently scan the area and are aware of what's taking place around them. They're always half looking for tracks, disturbances in the ground or changes in the behaviour of wildlife. This colour is the safest level to be in, and it adds to the enjoyment of being outdoors. In the old days, most people who lived in rural areas or spent time in the woods acted this way as a matter of course. Today, it's often referred to as being in the present moment.

The third colour is orange, which means tracks have been seen, something has been smelled or heard or a person suddenly gets a funny feeling. This is the time to carefully observe the environment and consider the next step, such as leaving the area, alerting others to the possible presence of a cougar or preparing your defence. No matter how uneasy or frightened you feel, you need to stop, stay calm and assess the situation. The final colour of awareness is red: you and the cougar see each other and it doesn't run away.

Assess the cougar's behaviour as it reacts to your responses and prepare for an attack.

If you spend time in cougar country, taking an awareness and safety course is highly recommended. Some community colleges,

In Dave Eyer's Bear & Cougar Encounters course, people learn how to respond to predators and receive hands-on training in the use of bear spray, knives and other weapons while cardboard cutouts (such as the bear pictured here) charge them at real-life speeds. *Photo by Johanna Bos*

schools and recreation centres offer them. If possible, attend a class that includes a field day where you can practise mock encounters similar to the way paramedics and firefighters are trained using simulated scenarios. Having a life-size cardboard cut-out of a cougar charging you at seventy-two kilometres (forty-five miles) per hour gives you an incredibly clear idea of how fast a predator can approach and is a good way to practise using inert bear spray, knives and other deterrents. It's also a good way to get the adrenaline going and find out how you might respond in an actual situation. On my first encounter with a cardboard cougar I screamed, closed my eyes and aimed the bear spray to the side. A real cougar would have had me on the ground in seconds. Needless to say, a course with both a classroom session and a field component is incredibly valuable and a real confidence booster.

"There will most likely always be some cougars that will attack humans if given the opportunity," said Dave Eyer. "People don't need to be frightened and looking over their shoulder all the time. But they can be aware and carry the gear. An informed and prepared public should be able to keep many dangerous encounters from becoming attacks."

CHAPTER 10:
Children, Dogs & Cougars

Children are magnets for cougars.

—RICK JAMES, author and field archaeologist

As opportunists, cougars are always on the lookout for an easy meal. Most of the time they don't see people as prey, but certain situations change that dynamic. Anything that is small, makes high-pitched sounds or moves quickly or erratically will attract their attention. That's why children and domestic dogs are of special concern when in cougar habitat. Their size and movements resemble the cat's natural prey, thus making them more vulnerable. A child, alone or in a group of children, is fourteen times more at risk of being attacked than an adult and there are many accounts of cougars killing dogs. But there are ways to mitigate the risk.

In October 1941, twenty-three-year-old Ruth Dickson was folding laundry in the bedroom while her four-month-old daughter napped in her buggy on the veranda. The family had moved into a duplex in the Sayward Valley on northern Vancouver Island fifteen months before. "My mind was on an unopened parcel of books from the library outreach program," Dickson wrote in her memoir, *Pebbles in the Stream.*

"Then I glanced out the window to see the buggy moving slightly. June was awake and talking to herself. 'Darn it! No time for books,' I was thinking, when another movement caught my attention. This one was across the garden beyond the picket fence. As I watched, a cougar arched in a leap over the gate. It was a young male, curious about the small cooing and chirping sounds he could hear near the house. He came slowly up the walk, head raised, intent on the sounds. With his front feet on the top step he paused, watching the slightly moving buggy.

"The long barreled .22 was handy and the loaded clip was right on the dresser. I was at the door in seconds. There was no time to think. At the shock of a burning sting in the skin at the top of his shoulders, the cougar somersaulted backwards. With two immense springs, he vaulted the gate and was gone in the woods across the road. I dropped the gun to the floor immediately after firing it through the screen door. I had my baby in my arms and was back in the house when our neighbour, Big Tim, thundered through the connecting door."

The cougar was drawn to the sounds the baby was making and perhaps the movement of the buggy. Dickson averted disaster by keeping a close eye on her daughter, being aware of what was going on and acting quickly at the first sign of danger.

Many parents have saved their children from harm by responding in the same way. Seven-year-old Kyle Musselman was only 45 metres (148 feet) from the elementary school in Gold River on northern Vancouver Island when a cougar attacked him on May 9, 1994. His friends threw rocks at the cat while his brother ran home for help. Musselman's dad, John, leapt out of bed, pulled on shorts and raced down the street barefoot. When he saw the thirty-six-kilogram (eighty-pound) male cougar standing over his son's bloody body, he bared his teeth, yelled and charged. The cat relinquished its prey.

In August 1996, when a cougar pulled her youngest son off his horse near Princeton, BC, thirty-six-year-old Cindy Parolin didn't hesitate. She dismounted and tackled the beast, yelling for her three children to get away. She saved her children but lost her own life doing so. While sledding at Danskin, BC, on December 31, 2009, seven-year-old David Metzler was attacked by a thirty-kilogram (sixty-six-pound) cougar. When his mother, who was tidying up the nearby church, heard the screams she rushed outside and hit the cougar with the only weapon she had—a cleaning cloth. One whack and the cat took off.

Children are magnets for cougars. It's almost as if the cat sees them as a different species than adult humans. And in a way, they are. They're smaller, tend to move quickly and erratically, and have higher-pitched voices. All that makes them appear like easy prey to take down. In the 2011 report "Factors Governing Risk of Cougar Attacks on Humans," the authors determined that even if a child was with adults, their chance of being attacked was more than six times higher than that of adults in the group. And the odds of an encounter escalating into an attack increased if one or more children were present in a group of adults. Children are also more likely than adults to die from a cougar attack.

Cougar safety literature advises parents to keep their kids close. But how close is close enough? On April 15, 2006, Shir Feldman was heading back to the family vehicle after a hike on Flagstaff Mountain Trail near Boulder, Colorado. His parents and two brothers were with him. The group was about forty-six metres (fifty yards) from the parking lot when a female mountain lion pounced on Shir. The seven-year-old was holding his dad's hand at the time. The family yelled and pelted the cat with sticks and rocks until it released the boy.

cougar jumped out of the bushes and buried its teeth in the back of his head. When Moore screamed his siblings started yelling at the cat. His brother hit it repeatedly with a shovel he found at the side of the trail while his sister slapped the cougar in the face with her stringer of fish. The children were able to repel the cat.

Some schools provide cougar awareness and defence sessions for their students but all children in cougar habitat need to be educated about the possibility of encountering the predator. The information should be presented in a matter-of-fact way, similar to teaching a child how to safely cross busy streets. The basics are: don't run, stare the cougar in the eye, act aggressive, fight back and help each other. "There's no need to make children fearful," said Dave Eyer. "Just let them know what to do. Teach school children to alert the playground supervisor if they spot a cougar. And tell them what to do if one approaches."

Playing in groups is best. Wearing a lanyard with a loud whistle on it when in or at the edge of wooded, brushy areas is a good idea, too, and a dog is often useful as an early warning system that a predator is nearby. Dogs frequently smell, hear or sense the presence of wild animals sooner than humans. A dog's incredible sense of smell and a human's eyesight can be a great combination when it comes to predator awareness. Adults and children should learn to read and pay attention to their dog's body language and actions. If Fido is on high alert, chances are they should be too. Tell children what to do if a pet starts exhibiting unusual behaviour.

Unless they're habituated, cougars probably perceive domestic dogs as some sort of wild canine. Out of all the canids, cougars have a particularly complex relationship with wolves. Cougars can and do kill individual wolves, in some cases frequently. But when a pack, with its coordinated chase and attack tactics, is involved, wolves definitely have the upper paw. Wolves kill kittens

In March 2013, Lori Iverson, the outdoor recreation planner for the National Elk Refuge in Wyoming, watched as two mountain lion cubs sought refuge on a buck and rail fence for over an hour while a small pack of coyotes harassed them. The cubs, estimated to be five- to six-months old, eventually escaped. *Photo by Lori Iverson, U.S. Fish and Wildlife Service*

and adult cougars and it's not unusual for a pack to roust a cougar off its kill. Even a lone barking coyote has been known to convince a cougar to abandon a prey carcass. If wolves are nearby, most cougars will leave the area or, at the very least, be extremely wary. They can easily escape their tormentors by climbing a tree. But wolves have been known to wait a cougar out until it gets too cold or weak to defend itself.

Many cougars won't turn and fight one or more barking dogs unless cornered or defending cubs. Most of the time when it comes to canines, a cougar's instinct is flight not fight. The problem is, due to their small lung capacity, cougars can't run far. So they climb trees. For most cats, unless the hounds stick around too long or a hunter with a rifle is following behind, a tree proves a safe haven.

But cougar hounds can be fanatically fervent about their vocation. While hunting cougars in Colorado during the early part of the twentieth century, Theodore Roosevelt's letters to his children often mentioned "dogs that climbed trees." There was Turk, a bloodhound who once followed a cougar almost nine metres (thirty feet) up a pinyon tree. And Tony, a young half-breed bulldog who pursued nearly every cat that went up a tree and regularly tumbled to the ground from six metres (twenty feet) or more. Apparently the branches and snow broke the dogs' falls, as they were always eager to chase another cat up a tree.

Just because a cougar trees doesn't mean it will stay there. After a short rest, some will jump down and run again. Winston Vickers, associate veterinarian at the UC Davis Wildlife Health Center, recalled one such incident when tracking mountain lions in San Diego County, California, around 2005. "We were just about to dart a lion with a tranquilizer when it jumped out of the tree and landed in the middle of the dog pack," he said. "In one smooth motion it leapt out of the tree, picked up a dog by the head and bounded off with it. Of course, all the hounds chased it. One caught up to the lion and grabbed it by the tail. That was enough to make it drop the dog, which survived but wasn't keen on chasing lions for a while."

Wildlife experts are often asked whether a dog is a deterrent or attractant to cougars. The answer depends on the cougar, the dog and the situation. Some cougars are frightened of dogs. But a young, inexperienced cougar or a starving, sick one may be desperate enough to attempt an attack. A mature, healthy cougar might not be able to resist the temptation of what looks like an easy meal. And for a cougar with a history of stalking and killing household pets, a dog is definitely an attractant.

"A large dog can look formidable to a cougar," said Dave Eyer. "But if the dog acts cowardly, tries to run, whines or hides behind their owner, those signals tell the cougar the dog is not a threat. If

Four year old Rudy climbs every tree he can after cougars. His owner, Doug McMann of Skinner Creek Hunts, said he tries to discourage his dogs from going up trees but the desire to catch a cat often overwhelms them. Rudy was about three metres (ten feet) off the ground in this photo; some of McMann's dogs have managed to climb as high as seven metres (twenty-five feet). *Photo by Steve Austin*

the dog stands squarely facing the cougar, barks and pulls at the leash trying to get at it, that tells the cougar, 'Don't tangle with this person and dog!'"

Eyer added, "If the dog chases the cougar and trees it, that's good. The person and dog have an opportunity to get away and it may teach the cat not to mess with people and dogs. If the cougar doesn't run, the dog may be seriously injured or killed. That keeps the person safe but is difficult to witness. In that case, a person has to make a judgement call as to whether they can safely intervene or not. That's a good time to have a can of bear spray on your belt."

The reality is most people don't expect to meet a cougar let alone deal with an aggressive one. In the late 1990s, Summer McGee and her partner hiked to Ripple Rock, a scenic lookout on eastern Vancouver Island. "When we got to the bluff we let Amber off leash and ate lunch," said McGee. "She stayed right by us until we started to leave then ran off the side of the rock."

That was unusual behaviour for the cocker spaniel. "I saw something brown and thought it was another dog," explained McGee. "Then Amber whimpered and I realized it was a cougar ten feet away, lying down with its paws over our dog. I didn't know what to do. The week before a woman [Cindy Parolin] had been killed defending her child from a cougar."

McGee and her partner decided not to take the cougar on. "The most awful thing was listening to our dog scream as we walked away. It was extremely difficult and painful," she said. Two men also hiking the trail tried to rescue the dog but later caught up with the women and said there was no way the cat would relinquish its prey.

As difficult as it was, McGee made the right decision. People have been killed attempting to rescue their pets from predators. "Human life must come first," said Eyer. "People need to be prepared to defend their dog but only to the degree that it is safe for them. They should stand back, use bear spray, throw rocks, scream and jab it with a stick from a distance, but never attempt to put themselves between the dog and cougar."

Even well-trained dogs should be leashed in high-risk areas. "Pets are an attractant to large carnivores," explained wildlife biologist Danielle Thompson. "If a dog is off leash that puts it in a whole different risk category. Despite that, a lot of people feel it's a personal affront to their freedom if you ask them to leash their dog. But a domestic dog is not an equal adversary to a wild animal that relies on hunting and killing to survive. You have a chance of protecting your dog when it's on leash. But if it's running free it is more likely to be singled out by a predator as a potential source of food."

"It's difficult to leash your dog on a big beach," she acknowledged. "But even though you don't see them, predators can be nearby. Recently some interns were out in the field and saw an adult bear on Long Beach. One girl was from Germany. Seeing a bear was a big deal for her so they watched it. The next thing they knew a wolf ran out and chased the bear off. Everyone was shocked because the wolf had been close to them all along but no one had noticed it."

For Dave Weighell, having his dogs on leash probably saved their lives. The thirty-seven-year-old was taking Sequoia, a border collie–husky cross, and Chinook, a large collie–Staffordshire terrier cross, on their regular late-night walk on March 2, 2012. Around midnight he was about 50 metres (164 feet) from his Canmore, Alberta condo. Suddenly a full-grown cougar grabbed the twenty-kilogram (forty-five-pound) Sequoia, the smaller dog, by the face and tried to pull the dog to the ground. Both dogs were on leash so everything was happening right in front of Weighell. He yelled and kicked the cat until it took off. Sequoia had a puncture wound but survived.

But not all dogs are as lucky. In March 2013, a dachshund was being walked by its owner in a gated community in Colorado when a cougar suddenly appeared, jerked the leash out of the man's hand and killed the dog. "In our area we've had cougars attack dogs at homes and dogs attack cougars at homes," said Dave Eyer, who lives in the BC Interior. "At one neighbour's, tracks clearly showed a cougar had walked around the barn, ignoring the calf and cow, gone around the chickens and hid under the house waiting for the dogs to be let out in the morning."

People with livestock and pets that don't sleep in the house need to ensure their animals have a safe enclosure at night. Cougars can leap great distances so secure barns and covered runs with strong wire tops are recommended. Walter Boyce, wildlife veterinarian and professor at UC Davis, considers mountain lions similar to human teenagers in some ways. "They're generally well behaved but they are also very good at finding ways to get into trouble," he said. "And there are plenty of ways for lions living near people to get into trouble. Given too much opportunity, lions eat domestic animals at some point—it just happens.

"If people let their livestock or pets run loose at night in lion habitat, that's an incredible temptation over time," Boyce added. "And once a lion kills livestock it is often destroyed. People need to recognize that their personal choices affect their domestic animals and the wild animals that live in the area."

But despite the risks, a well-trained, obedient dog can be a valuable asset when it comes to personal defence. "The dog must stay within fiftee metres of the owner to act as the human's keen ears and nose," Dave Eyer wrote in his *Bear & Cougar Encounters Course Handbook.* "The dog must heel on command and come when called—even if it prefers to face off with a predator. It must not attack unless ordered to do so. Though training is important, be aware that some dogs have it and some don't. A dog that has a strong bond with its owner will be willing to protect and fight for them if need be."

And that's what saved Austin Forman from injury and perhaps death. As the eleven-year-old pushed the wheelbarrow back and forth between the woodshed and his house he wondered why Angel was sticking so close. The eighteen-month-old golden retriever usually ran around in the snow sniffing and playing. It was January 3, 2010, and, at 5:30 p.m., already dark. Forman was a metre (a few feet) away from the woodshed when he saw another dog. But as it moved into the glow of the yard light he realized it was a cougar. In mid-leap.

Before Forman could react Angel jumped between him and the cat. The boy ran into the house where everyone could hear Angel making horrible noises. Forman's mom, Sherri, called 911. Luckily Boston Bar, BC, is a small community and the RCMP office was only a block away. Constable Chad Gravelle raced to the Forman house where he learned Austin was okay but the cougar had dragged Angel under the deck steps.

With his flashlight Gravelle saw the dog and cougar tangled together in the small space. He shot at the cougar's rear end hoping to sever its spine. When that didn't work he shifted his position. Now only two metres (six feet) away, he glimpsed part of the cougar's head behind Angel's. He pulled the trigger. The cougar died with its jaws clamped around Angel's muzzle, trying to suffocate her. When Forman's cousin retrieved the dog from under the steps, Angel was covered in blood and motionless. Then she inhaled deeply, struggled to her feet and ran over to sniff Forman. Although badly chewed up around the head, Angel made a full recovery. Without her presence, Forman surely would have been mauled, or worse. And without the quick response of Constable Gravelle, Angel would have died.

While conducting research for "Factors Governing Risk of Cougar Attacks on Humans," the authors discovered that time of day and location played a strong role in whether a dog was an attractant or a deterrent to a cougar. Walking with a dog on a trail or road during daylight decreased the odds of a person experiencing a close encounter. However, a dog outside a residence or camp at night placed a person at increased risk, as darkness created an opportunity for a cougar to sneak up near a house or campsite, and owners were sometimes injured while attempting to rescue their pet.

Just because a person is out with their dog during the day doesn't mean they should forget about scanning their surroundings and paying attention to what's going on. Suzanne Olszowiec was walking her three cattle-herding dogs along the Puntledge River pipeline trail on central Vancouver Island one afternoon in October 2011. When two women and their labs approached, she called her dogs. As they ran up and were being leashed, Olszowiec heard a low growling sound. A cougar, about the size of a big German shepherd, was in the bushes about two metres (seven feet) away. "I could see its lips moving," she said. "The dogs were running around and vocalizing so it was watching them. But I got the feeling if the dogs hadn't been there, it would have been watching the people." None of the five dogs noticed the cougar.

From that point on, Olszowiec began carrying bear bangers and a half-kilogram (twenty-ounce) framing hammer or heavy flashlight with her when she walked the dogs. The following spring she saw what she suspects was the same cougar. Her dogs were about nine metres (thirty feet) in front of her when all of a sudden everything went quiet. "There wasn't even any bird noise," she said. "I glanced behind me and a cougar was on the road. It looked at me then went into a farmer's field.

"Perhaps the wind was wrong because the dogs didn't notice the cougar that time either," she added. "The cougar looked a little older and bigger and a lot less afraid of people. I'd be happy to never see it again but that's a part of life around here. And even though I've only seen this cougar twice, I'm sure he's seen me a hundred and two times."

When it comes to dogs and cougars and who chases who, it may be a matter of which animal sees the other first. If a cougar is stalking a dog or a person—some cougars go for the dog, others attack people and show no interest whatsoever in the dog, whether it's a corgi or a St. Bernard—it may not run away when noticed. On the other hand, if a cougar is surprised by a barking, charging dog, its first instinct might be to get the heck out of there. A medium- to large-size dog is generally more of a deterrent than a small one and two dogs are better than one.

"I don't know why some lions run from dogs and others attack them," admitted Winston Vickers. "I think it depends on the circumstances and the individual lion. Sometimes if they're around rural areas with livestock lions can become used to dogs. But in some cases a little dog can put a cat up a tree all by itself."

And that's sort of what happened one night in May 2009, when Philomath, Oregon, resident Loren Wingert heard her small border terrier squealing in the yard. When she looked outside she saw a mountain lion pinning Rosie to the ground. Wingert ran to the phone to call for help, but it was already there. Her tiny chihuahua, Chiquita, barked its heart out until the lion dropped Rosie and left the yard.

Less than a month later, Analee Spray's dogs couldn't wait to get out of their Riverside County home in southern California. Spray, along with her three-year-old daughter, followed the barking trio to the garage. When she peeked inside, Spray saw a mountain lion. The toy chihuahuas, weighing just over a kilogram (three pounds) each, held the large cat at bay for forty-five minutes until a Fish and Wildlife official arrived.

When it comes to cougars, attitude is important. And in some cases, it can even make up for size and strength. Dogs can be a good early warning system, distract a nearby cougar and defend their owner if a cat attacks. And even young children can deter a cougar if they know what to do and have someone to help them.

CHAPTER 11:
Cougar Attack Hot Spots

There is a history of cougars attacking and consuming
people... and it happens more on Vancouver Island
than any other place in North America.
—BOB HANSEN, wildlife specialist, *Canadian Geographic*

Cougars are mysterious, magnificent creatures. Their stealthy nature allows them to pass through forests, deserts and urban neighbourhoods unseen and to sneak up on their prey without a sound. They are built to kill, and do so extremely well. But while the majority of cougars prey on deer and other animals, some attack humans. And in certain regions of Canada and the US, this happens much more frequently than in other locations.

Around 7:00 p.m. on August 1, 2002, David Parker was walking to the Jeune Landing industrial log-sorting depot a couple of kilometres (a little over a mile) from his home in Port Alice, BC. Located on northern Vancouver Island, the community has about eight hundred residents, most making a living in the logging industry or working at the pulp mill. Parker's a regular walker and he particularly enjoyed taking this route on a summer evening. "You often see a really nice sunset from the dry-sort," he said.

About a half an hour into the outing a rain squall blew in off the inlet. Parker's short-sleeved shirt and jeans didn't offer much protection so he ducked under a rock overhang and leaned back to wait the rain out. The next thing he knew, a cougar's fangs were less than an arm's length from his head. "Just before the attack I heard a soft plop plop sound like snow falling from a tree limb and striking the ground," he said. "It was the cougar's paws on the rock above me. As soon as I saw it, I instinctively raised my left shoulder to protect my neck."

The force of the impact knocked the sixty-one-year-old face down on the gravel logging road, shattering his left temple, eye socket, cheek bone and jaw. He felt a floating sensation, then the pain of his scalp being shredded. A piece of it fell forward and blood dripped from his hair. "The cougar was on my back so I put my hands behind my neck to protect it," Parker explained. "Then the cougar bit into my skull—the pressure was enormous—it was crushing, scooping out a piece of my head. Despite the excruciating pain, I knew if I didn't do something soon I'd die." He reached for the folding knife in the sheath on his belt. But as soon as his hand moved, the cat went for his neck. Realizing his mistake, Parker snapped his head to the side. The cougar bit into the right side of his face, peeling it back from his nose to his ear, which was left hanging by a thread of skin. His eye, along with some attached muscles and socket pieces, dangled on his cheek by the optical nerve. "At that moment I thought my life was over and decided to inflict as much damage as I could."

Despite having his head on the down side of the hill and a forty-five-kilogram (one-hundred pound) cougar on his back, the retired millworker used his arms to lift his body up. "I just kept pushing, pushing as hard as I could against the gravel," he said. "Finally I got my knees under me and pushed back as hard and fast

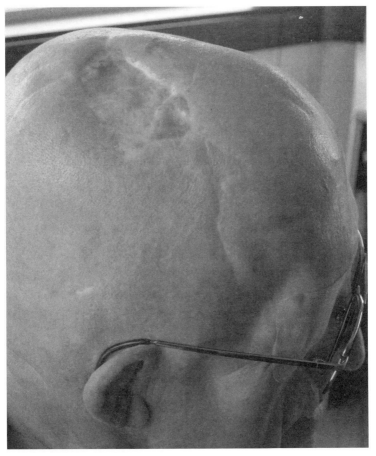

Despite the excruciating pain and pressure of a full-grown cougar's canine teeth puncturing and crushing his skull, David Parker knew he had to fight back or die. *Photo by Paula Wild*

as I could." As they toppled backwards, the cat scampered clear, then charged. Parker swivelled on his butt to kick it in the face. "It came at me again and again, it was relentless," he said. "My feet were bruised from kicking it so hard. I was yelling obscenities and it was making a yowling noise." Once when the cougar swatted at him he grabbed it by the forepaw but it quickly twisted free.

Another time it ran between his legs and he gripped it in a scissor hold but it squirmed loose.

Then Parker grabbed the cougar again. "I got a grip just back of its forelegs, put my chin into its chest and held on," he said. The cougar thrashed and squirmed. "He hated being held like that but I squeezed as hard as I could. I just kept pushing and squeezing until the cougar was standing on its back toes." But as soon as he eased up on the pressure, the fight resumed. Parker knew he had to go for his knife again. This time he managed to get it out but lost it in the scuffle. "The cougar was on me and I was trying to hold it away," he said. "Then I felt the smoothness of the knife under the back of my right hand and grabbed it." He let go of the cougar to open the folding knife. And dropped it again. The fight continued. When Parker found the knife a second time he knew it was his last chance.

While Parker was opening the knife, the cougar dug its right foreclaws into his shoulder. Parker swung the blade at the paw, stabbing himself instead. "I couldn't really see—my left eye was full of blood and dirt from the cougar bite and wrestling around on the ground, and my right eye was bobbling uselessly on my face," he said. "With my right elbow on the cougar's chest I took two quick jabs towards its head." By luck, he stabbed it in the jugular vein each time. The cougar went wild. Even with blood spurting from its neck it still fought. Parker hugged the cat to him as hard as he could in an attempt to minimize the damage. "When it stopped moving I let go," he said. "But it jerked to life again so I had to hold it for at least another minute."

When Parker stood up he saw two huge pools of blood on the ground: one his, the other the cougar's. He threw the knife at the cat and staggered a kilometre and a half (a mile) down the road toward the dry-land sorting depot. It was closer than home and he could hear equipment operating. He went to the machine

Trying to get the folding knife (shown at bottom) open while a cougar attacked him almost cost David Parker his life. Now he doesn't even go into his own backyard without a fixed-blade knife (top) in a sheath on his belt.
Photo by Paula Wild

shed where some fellows had been working the evening before but it was locked. Farther away someone was cleaning up the grounds on an excavator. By this time it was getting dark. Parker threw a chunk of wood at the machine to get the driver's attention. Jeff Reaume took one look at the blood-soaked man and sped him to the Port Alice Hospital.

Parker and his wife, Helen, spent the next two years visiting hospitals as he underwent extensive reconstructive surgery. He knows if he had lost the sight of both eyes on the logging road, or not found the knife the second time, he wouldn't be around today. The couple still lives in Port Alice, and Parker goes for walks most days but never outside the village alone.

"Everything has changed," he said. "My right eye doesn't work and I have trouble with my right ear and nostril. I have three steel plates in my head and a big dent in my skull where the cougar bit me." Parker never leaves the house—even to go into the backyard—without a fixed-blade knife on his belt. "All my injuries occurred before I got the knife out," he explained. "The conservation officer told me I was lucky the blade was so sharp. He said most knives aren't sharp enough to cut through a cougar's hide."

As for the cougar, a post-mortem exam revealed it was a healthy three- to four-year-old male that had eaten within twelve hours of the attack. Although Parker's a tall, fit man, he was alone, and ducking under the rock overhang may have made him appear smaller and thus more vulnerable. Healthy, mature cougars attack humans less frequently than young cats but, due to their size and hunting expertise, the encounters are more often fatal. The fact that a 77-kilogram (170-pound) man, unarmed for much of the altercation, was able to fight off an animal capable of taking down a full-grown elk is a true testament to Parker's resourcefulness and will to survive.

Soon after the attack, Parker watched walkers pass his home armed with knives, bear spray and walking sticks. But ten years later few carry any defensive weapons. "People forget," he said. "They think it won't happen to them. But my wife and I, we never forget. Not even for a day."

In 2002, Parker had lived in Port Alice for twenty years. He knew cougars were around but had only begun carrying a knife eighteen months before the attack. And he'd done so because of what happened to John Nostdal on February 8, 2001. Around 9:30 p.m., the Seattle resident was riding his bike from the Port Alice townsite back to his boat near the pulp mill when he noticed a clicking noise similar to fingernails tapping on a hard surface and thought something was loose on his backpack. Then a heavy weight hit the fifty-two-year-old from behind, knocking him to the ground. Suddenly the big, strong tugboat owner was fighting for his life. The cougar kept trying to bite his neck but Nostdal's jacket and backpack, which had his yoga mat in it, were in the way.

Elliot Cole was driving home from the mill when he saw a man on the ground covered in blood. Initially he thought it was a biking accident. Then he saw the cougar. Without thinking, Cole leapt out of his truck and began yelling and hitting the cougar with a bag of binders. When that didn't work, he punched the animal in the head a few times. But the cougar wouldn't give up. Cole grabbed Nostdal's bike and used it to pin the cat to the ground while yelling at Nostdal to get in the truck. Cole punched the cougar so hard its head bounced off the pavement and he joined Nostdal in the vehicle. Even then the cougar held its ground, only leaving when Cole stomped on the gas pedal. Nostdal is convinced that his backpack, his yoga mat and Cole's timely appearance and brave actions saved his life. Wildlife officials believed the cougar might have been the same one that had recently survived being hit by a car, confronted a local resident and killed several pets.

Overall, cougar sightings are infrequent, encounters rare, and attacks extremely so. Yet it seems like everyone who has lived on Vancouver Island any length of time has a cougar story to tell, and often two or three. Most are of fleeting glimpses of a long tail arcing across the road in front of a vehicle late at night. That's a thrilling moment. But other stories are filled with emotional and physical trauma and sometimes death. In the last two hundred years, 89 of the 252 documented cougar attacks on humans have occurred in British Columbia. And 50 of those took place on Vancouver Island. That's pretty amazing considering that the island is just over three percent of the land mass of BC and less than one percent of current

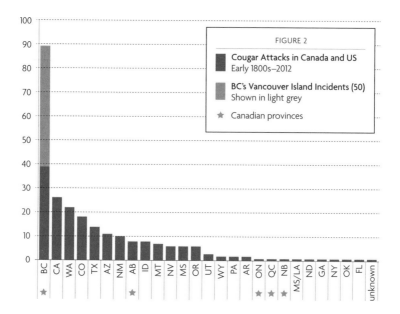

Chart prepared by David G. Eyer

cougar habitat in North America. In comparison, the next highest number of attacks, 26, took place in California.

At the end of 2012, the BC Ministry of Forests, Lands and Natural Resource Operations estimated there were six thousand cougars in the province, including six hundred on Vancouver Island. If those ratios were more or less constant over the years that would mean a mere ten percent of the BC cougar population was responsible for fifty-six percent of the attacks in province.

As well as having the highest number of attacks of anywhere in Canada and the US, Vancouver Island has the highest density of cougars. And that's despite extensive hunting. Some say cougars on the island have been the most aggressively hunted of any state or province. In *Island Gold,* Dell Hall noted that sixty percent of the cougars killed in BC during the bounty years came from Vancouver Island. After the bounty was dropped and cougars became a big game animal, forty-two percent of cougars killed in BC (as of 1990) were from the island. Obviously, the big cats have been able to hold their own and even increase their populations at times.

BC has some of the biggest cougars in the world—some weighing more than 225 pounds—but Vancouver Island has always had a reputation for the most aggressive ones. "West Coast cougars have a particularly nasty disposition," Hall wrote. And in *Panther,* Roderick Haig-Brown noted, "The black striped northern Vancouver Island cougars were the ones hunters most feared."

The number of attacks on the island vary from year to year but what's interesting, in a macabre sort of way, is where they've taken place. David Parker's 2002 encounter was the second incident in Port Alice within two years. And the sixth to occur between 2001 and 2005 in what Vancouver Island residents call the North Island, loosely defined as the area north of Campbell River and Gold River. Over the last two hundred years the North Island has been the site of thirty-one cougar attacks. That is twelve percent of all incidents in Canada and the US. And the attacks weren't just randomly scattered across the landscape. At Fort Rupert, a twenty-minute drive south of Port Hardy, one cougar killed twelve girls. In the vicinity of Port Alice and nearby Lake Victoria there have been seven attacks. The Port Hardy area, Gold River and Holberg have experienced three each and Quatsino Sound, Kyuquot and Zeballos have had two attacks each. Eight other locations have experienced one attack and there have been numerous occasions where cougars have stalked people and pets.

Beginning in 2011 the high frequency of cougar–human altercations shifted to the lower portion of the island. That year a cougar stalked a teenager in Nanaimo, and then over the Labour Day weekend a two-year-old healthy cougar was shot at Park

Sands Beach Resort near downtown Parksville and an eighteen-month-old cougar was killed at Goldstream Park, just north of Victoria. Both young animals were brazenly watching crowded campgrounds in broad daylight and showed no fear of humans, even when people shouted and threw rocks at them. A cougar killed a horse in the Comox Valley on the central east coast of Vancouver Island, and a woman in a rural area of Nanaimo found a cougar feeding on a deer in her backyard. Cougar sightings in the greater Victoria region included a kindergarten class that had to abandon their walk when they came across a cougar feeding on a kill.

Communities on the western side of the island also had some tense situations. In 2011, an eighteen-month-old boy was attacked at Swim Beach in the Kennedy Lake day-use area of Pacific Rim National Park Reserve. After the grandfather and a family friend rescued the boy, the cougar circled his four-year-old sister. A woman was stalked and threatened while jogging near Ucluelet. Farther up the peninsula, a man who broke off from a group walking on Cox Bay Beach was stalked and cougars were seen in the middle of the day at the Long Beach parking lot and the Tofino Crab Dock. The following year, a seven-year-old boy was attacked at Sproat Lake near Port Alberni in August and a month later a thirty-eight-year-old man was attacked at an Ahousaht gravel pit located on Flores Island, northwest of Tofino. Altogether, twelve Vancouver Island communities have been the site of more than one cougar attack in the last century.

Vancouver Island isn't the only place that seems to have unusually aggressive cougars. Like most of Canada and the US, California went through an intense bounty-hunting period, followed by the regulation of mountain lions as big game. In 1990 residents voted in favour of Proposition 117, making mountain lions a "specially protected species." According to the California Department of Fish and Wildlife, Proposition 117 makes it "illegal to take, injure, possess, transport, import, or sell any mountain lion or part of a mountain lion." They can only be killed if a depredation permit is issued for a specific lion attacking livestock or pets, to preserve public safety and to protect listed (endangered) bighorn sheep. A new policy allowing conservation officers more options to deal with potential human conflict was introduced in 2013. Aside from Florida, California is the only jurisdiction in the US or Canada to protect mountain lions to such an extent.

As of this book's publication, the most recent serious mountain lion attack in California took place on January 24, 2007. Fortuna, California, residents Jim and Nell Hamm were near the end of a sixteen-kilometre (ten-mile) trek in Prairie Creek Redwoods State Park, half a day's drive north of San Francisco. It was close to 3:00 p.m. and starting to get dark so they turned onto a shortcut to the parkway trailhead. "I heard a couple of little noises and then something louder like a bike behind me on the gravel path," recalled Jim. "I turned and a mountain lion was in mid-flight, paws straight out, coming right at me." The seventy-year-old quickly lowered his shoulder and turned to the side. The lion flew over him, turned and leapt at Hamm's upraised arm. "The lion had its teeth clamped on my arm and was dangling from it with all four paws in the air trying to get me," he said. "I tried to punch it but the cat was heavy and I fell down."

With Jim face down on the path, the lion ripped a piece of his scalp off. "Jim didn't scream," said Nell, who was about six metres (twenty feet) up the trail. "It was a different, horrible sound." When the sixty-five-year-old spun around she saw her husband laying on the trail with his head in the lion's jaws. "I don't remember looking for it but the next thing I knew, I was

After a mountain lion nearly killed Jim Hamm, he and his wife, Nell, were afraid to go on the long-distance hikes they loved. But over time they conquered their fear and now encourage others to be aware and alert and to carry bear spray and knives when in lion habitat. *Photo courtesy Jim and Nell Hamm*

holding a big redwood branch about four inches thick and eight feet long," Nell said. "It was winter so the log was wet and heavy. Even with the adrenaline flowing, it was all I could do to lift it." Afraid of hurting Jim, she hit the lion over and over on its torso, screaming "Fight, Jim! Fight!" with every blow.

"The branch was so heavy it bounced off Nell's legs every time she hit the lion," Jim said. "Her legs were black and blue afterwards but the cat never flinched." Jim shifted his body a bit, stuck his fingers in the lion's nose and twisted as hard as he could. "It let go of my head and grabbed me by the lips. We were teeth to teeth and I could see every cell in its eyes, they went from round to elongated. Then it shook its head, tearing my lips apart from my nose to my chin, exposing a large part of my mouth." When the lion went back to licking his head, Jim shoved his thumb in its eye with all the force he could muster. "A cat's eyes move around in the sockets and my thumb went sideways hitting bone. That's when I told Nell to get a pen out of my pocket and stab the lion in the eye right through to the brain."

"When Jim started talking it was a relief because I knew he was still alive," Nell remembered. "I thought the pen would go in easily but after about an inch it bent so I went back to hitting the cat with the log. I just knew it was going to kill Jim."

The lion kept biting Jim's skull and trying to shake him by the neck but his backpack was in the way. In desperation, Jim stuck his right hand in the cat's mouth. "It really hurt but its tongue was rubbery and I could get a good grip on it," he explained. "I know if you hold a dog's tongue they can't do anything. But that made the lion really mad so I had to release and grab again. Then it got loose and went back for my head."

"Jim told me to do something different," said Nell. "So even though I was worried about hurting him, I took the sharp end of the log and rammed it in the lion's face." The cat was holding onto Jim with its eyes closed, apparently waiting for him to die. But Nell's new tactic caused it to open its eyes and let go of Jim. It crouched two metres away (six feet) with its ears pinned back, glaring at Nell. "Jim's blood was all over her muzzle and chest," she said. "I knew she was going to attack so I raised the branch over my head and screamed as loud as I could, "She's got me, Jim! She's got me!" The lion hesitated then casually walked off into the ferns.

The fight had lasted about six minutes. Nell tried to get Jim up but he was bleeding profusely and in shock, and kept muttering that he was tired. But Nell knew that having so much blood around meant the cat would be back. Somehow she got Jim on his feet and they headed to the trailhead four hundred metres (a quarter mile) away. "Part of my scalp was left on the ground, the rest hung from my head," Jim said. "At one point we managed to jog a bit and I could feel it bouncing on my shoulders." When they reached the trailhead Nell laid Jim down and gathered some logs in case the lion followed them. Their cellphone wouldn't work so they had to wait for someone to come by. Jim's head and face were so badly mauled Nell couldn't bear to look at him.

Jim had lost a lot of blood and was treated for wounds to his head, hands and legs. His lips had to be sewn back together and a thin slice of muscle with a skin graft was needed to cover the large section of scalp that had been torn away. His wounds became infected and he nearly died. At the attack site, wildlife officials killed two lions. The larger of the two, a healthy but skinny two- to three-year-old female, had human blood under her claws.

The Hamms had always been active and athletic and they'd previously discussed what to do in the event of a mountain lion attack. But most importantly, like David Parker, they never gave up. Officials told them that if Jim had been by himself, he probably would have died. Nell is certain neither one of them would have survived if the attack had taken place earlier in the day. "Jim couldn't have gone very far and I never would have left him," she said.

Most mountain lions go to great lengths to avoid humans but when they do attack, it can be physically and emotionally devastating. In addition to Jim's long physical recovery, the Hamms had to deal with their fear. "During the attack I knew I was going to die," Jim said. "Afterwards, I was afraid to go outside. I thought about moving to the city but a person isn't necessarily safe there either. It took a lot of willpower and determination to go outside—our backyard borders onto redwood forest—but I didn't want to huddle in the house the rest of my life."

The Hamms have resumed taking long-distance hikes several times a week and have even revisited the site of the attack. "We're not afraid now, just aware," Jim said. "We both carry bear spray and knives. And we've spent a lot of time informing people about cougar attacks and encouraging them to be prepared and not hike alone."

California's earliest verified mountain lion attack occurred in 1870, and there were a total of nine by 1944. Then there was a stretch of forty-two years before the next one. That took place in Caspers Wilderness Park in Orange County, just outside of San Juan Capistrano in southern California. At about 2:00 p.m. on March 23, 1986, Laura Small was looking for tadpoles in a stream with her mother, Susan. The family had visited the park often and Laura's dad and nine-year-old brother were nearby. Suddenly, the five-year-old disappeared without a sound. Susan had glimpsed a "muscular animal" dragging her daughter away but it took a few moments for her to comprehend what had happened. Then she screamed as loud as she could. Laura's dad and brother came running, as well as some other hikers. They found Laura in some bushes with the mountain lion standing over her. One of the hikers brandished a stick at the cat while her parents grabbed her and ran.

Laura was in bad shape. In *Cat Attacks: True Stories and Hard Lessons from Cougar Country*, Jo Deurbrouck and Dean Miller wrote, "Her scalp, nose, and upper lip hung loose. Her right eye had been sliced open. Her skull had been crushed so severely that a portion of her brain had been liquefied by the pressure." Immediately after the attack Orange County closed Caspers Wilderness Park for a while and a two-year-old, healthy male lion was shot near the site of the incident. The Smalls successfully sued the county, citing numerous daytime sightings of mountain lions and aggressive behaviour by two cats during the months preceding Laura's attack, but no warning signs posted at the park to warn visitors. Then, on October 19 of the same year, six-year-old Justin Mellon was hiking with his parents and sister, as well as his uncle's family, in the park. Justin stopped to tie his shoelace and a mountain lion hit him so hard it knocked him out of his shoes. His dad, Tim, rushed the cougar with the fixed-blade knife he carried in a sheath. The cat dropped the boy but kept its eyes on him while his mother carried him away. Tim and his brother-in-law waved their arms in the air and yelled until the mountain lion walked away.

The Mellons also sued Orange County and settled out of court. This time the park was closed for three months. When it reopened, children, accompanied by adults, were only allowed in the picnic areas adjacent to the paved roadway. Warning signs about mountain lions were posted in prominent locations and updated after each sighting. Visitors were even asked to sign waivers before entering the park. Only a few declined to do so and left. Ten years later, in December 1997, children were once again allowed full access to the park. Within two weeks a group of hikers consisting of women and young children were charged by a mountain lion, which was later destroyed. Orange County was in a difficult position. No one wanted to close the park to children permanently and Californians were unlikely to condone the killing of all mountain lions in the area. As of 2013 the park has remained fully accessible to children and there have been no further incidents.

In 2004, attacks in Whiting Ranch Wilderness Park, about a thirty-minute drive from Caspers Wilderness Park, made the news. Thirty-year-old Anne Hjelle was mountain biking with her friend Debi Nicholls on Cactus Ridge Run on January 8 when a mountain lion knocked her off her bike around 4:30 p.m. The fitness instructor and former Marine fought back with everything she had but said afterward the lion possessed "the strength of ten men." She didn't know that just a short distance away and within the past twenty-four hours the cat had killed and partially eaten Mark Jeffrey Reynolds, a thirty-five-year-old competitive mountain bike racer.

The lion tried to bite the back of Hjelle's neck but when her helmet got in the way the cat shifted its teeth toward the side of her head. The mountain lion bit her face and neck, ripping her left ear from her skull and folding the left side of her cheek over her nose. As the mountain lion dragged Hjelle into the bush she heard Nicholls screaming and then felt her friend grab her leg. The forty-seven-year-old played a deadly game of tug-of-war with the mountain lion as it pulled both women farther from the trail. Then five other cyclists heard the ruckus. They threw rocks from the trail and when one hit it in the face, the lion released Hjelle but remained nearby. Hjelle was severely mauled but survived thanks to her friend's determination. A healthy two-year-old, 55-kilogram (122-pound) lion was later killed in the area. Tests revealed that it was responsible for both attacks.

But perhaps the spookiest series of California mountain lion skirmishes took place 121 kilometres (75 miles) away from Whiting Ranch Wilderness Park. In 1993 and 1994, mountain lions in Rancho Cuyamaca State Park chased horseback riders, bit a ten-year-old girl, mauled a dog, threatened three cyclists and almost attacked a three-year-old boy. In the last incident, when five park officials, accompanied by two dogs, found the cat they said it showed no fear of humans. Some of the problem mountain lions were juveniles and one had a deer carcass stashed nearby. But it was a healthy 59-kilogram (130-pound) male about five years old that killed fifty-six-year-old Iris M. Kenna on December 10, 1994, as she hiked in the park alone.

The lions in Rancho Cuyamaca Park were getting such a bad reputation that even park rangers were wary of walking the trails alone. People living nearby felt that going to the park meant entering the food chain. Throughout the 1990s there were eighteen occasions when lions acted aggressively toward humans, including two attacks and one fatality. Between 1993 and 1998 wildlife officials killed twelve lions due to public safety concerns. Park maps even carried warnings that Cuyamaca lions were known to be unusually aggressive. But that didn't deter people from enjoying the tranquillity and beauty of the area.

Lucy Oberlin had been running in the park for seventeen years when she encountered a mountain lion in August 1997. Oberlin and her long-time friend Diane Shields were halfway through a 22.5-kilometre (14-mile) run when they spotted the animal. As the cat trotted toward them the women yelled and waved their arms. When it didn't stop, one of them used her pepper spray. The spray didn't make contact with the cat's face but did make the cat back up. The women edged over to a stand of small trees just as the lion charged. Oberlin waved a big stick and Shields threw rocks. For fifteen minutes the cat charged again and again, coming in fast and low then retreating. But each time it came a little bit closer. The women yelled constantly, even when talking to each other, but the lion never made a sound. Shields started to go into shock and Oberlin yelled at her to bring her around. Then the lion charged and didn't stop. This time it got a squirt of spray in the face. It retreated but refused to leave. Slowly the women moved from tree to tree until they reached their vehicle in the parking lot.

Despite their ordeal, Oberlin and Shields still ran in the park. Four mountain lions were shot soon after their report and they figured their odds of seeing another one were extremely low. Just in case, Oberlin bought a .380 handgun to carry in her fanny pack. They avoided the trail where they'd met the cat for about a year. Then one day they included it on their run. They'd just passed a bunch of children at an outdoor camp when Oberlin saw a mountain lion across the river watching them. It shadowed them for half a kilometre (a third of a mile). Oberlin got her gun out but decided not to shoot unless it crossed the river. Even then she wasn't sure she'd be able to use the gun due to their proximity to the highway. Once again the women made it to safety.

In 2001, in response to all the negative encounters, the UC Davis Wildlife Health Center was hired to study how mountain lions and people shared the landscape at Rancho Cuyamaca State Park. The team fitted lions with GPS collars capable of tracking their movements hourly and monitored visitor and lion use of trails. The results of the study were pretty much what researchers expected and consistent with research in other areas: male mountain lions covered larger distances than females and both sexes were most active on or near trails just before and after dawn and dusk and throughout the night. Those were the times when the mountain lions did most of their hunting. In general, the lions were farthest away from human activity areas during the daytime.

But they weren't a great distance away. Eight out of thirty-three prey caches were located within 100 metres (109 yards) of a trail and two were within 300 metres (328 yards) of human structures such as campgrounds, park headquarters and residences for park employees. The study revealed that during the day adult lions could be expected to be within 100 metres (109 yards) of a trail nearly a quarter of the time they were within park boundaries. None seemed to be overly attracted to areas used by humans and none showed any aggression. In fact, the study indicated the lions were going out of their way to avoid people. The most likely time for altercations was around sunset when people were often still on the trails and the lions were becoming more active.

"It's interesting that as soon as the study started there was no further aggression by mountain lions," said Winston Vickers, associate veterinarian at the Wildlife Health Center. "Back in the nineties, in Cuyamaca and a park in Orange Country, there were several incidents of aggression. But nothing like that has happened in Cuyamaca since then and only one incident has occurred in Orange County. So to say mountain lions in either area are inherently aggressive does not appear to be accurate. That sort of activity is so rare. There can be a cluster of aggressive behaviour and then nothing for decades. Lions ignore people ninety-nine point nine per cent of the time—they just let us go by or sneak away."

Just as individual cougars exhibit different behaviour, so can cougar populations within a particular geographic location. For instance, researchers studying mountain lions in New Mexico were able to approach within fifty metres (fifty-five yards) of lions on 256 occasions and only observed threatening responses 16 times. On the other hand, in the past 31 years there have been 14 mountain lion attacks in Texas, with 11 of them occurring in Big Bend National Park. Unfortunately, it's impossible to tell if there is an aggressive cougar in an area. Cougars that attack humans are often killed and the problem goes away. But since there's no way to tell if another aggressive cougar has recently moved in to claim the vacant territory, it is best to always be aware and prepared, especially in regions with a history of aggressive cougars.

The frequency of attacks and fatalities in different regions of western Canada and the western US is baffling in its diversity. In the last two hundred years, California has been the site of twenty-six attacks with eight fatalities, Oregon has had six attacks with no fatalities and Washington has had twenty-two attacks and two deaths. During the same time period in Canada, Alberta had eight attacks resulting in one fatality and of the eighty-nine attacks in BC, twenty were fatalities. The fifty BC incidents that occurred on Vancouver Island led to seventeen deaths. Out of the eight fatalities in California, five were adults. In contrast, out of the twenty fatalities in BC, nineteen were children and teenagers, seventeen of which were killed on Vancouver Island.

BC, VANCOUVER ISLAND & CALIFORNIA ATTACKS AND FATALITIES 1812–2012

ATTACKS

BC Attacks: 89

56% (50)
on Vancouver Island

44% (39)
other areas of BC

California Attacks: 26

FATALITIES

BC Fatalities by Location:

85% (17)
Vancouver Island

15% (3)
other BC areas

100% (17) of fatalities on Vancouver Island
were 19 or younger

67% (2) of fatalities in
other areas of BC
were 19 or younger

33% (1) of fatalities in
other areas of BC
were 20 years or older

California Fatalities by age

37% (3) were 19 or younger

63% (5) were 20 or older

(rounded to nearest percentage)

So why are there so many attacks on the island? Both California and Vancouver Island enjoy a temperate climate and have experienced large increases in human population. And improved infrastructure often means parks and wilderness areas are only a short distance away from residential areas. On the island, logging roads have made remote areas more accessible than ever before. But Vancouver Island has always had more attacks, even when there were fewer roads and humans. And in the United States, radio-collared mountain lions have been tracked in high-density human habitation and yet remained largely unnoticed and did not attack anyone. So something else must be going on.

Wildlife officials and scientists have various theories about the aggressive tendencies of Vancouver Island cougars. Information obtained from the BC Ministry of Forests, Lands and Natural Resource Operations (FLNRO) noted there is a high density of cougars on the north end of the island but the habitat isn't the best for deer and elk and there are lower populations of small prey such as raccoons. As the deer population fluctuates, cougars either have enough to eat or may become desperate enough to attack humans. The spike of cougar complaints in the 1990s coincided with a large crash of the local deer population.

The ministry also pointed out that the broken rock, steep ground and dense vegetation on the North Island provides prime stalking cover. Indeed, in places the brush is so thick a person could be right next to a cougar and not know it. Other factors FLNRO mentioned that may trigger aggression included a high density of cats resulting in more territory overlap, increased fighting among males and more adult males killing kittens, as well as a high population of wolves consistently running cougars off their kills. All these stressors have the potential to affect cougar health and behaviour.

Data from FLNRO also noted, "Aggressive cats are generally younger ones that have a hard time making kills and/or are severely emaciated. This can degrade their physical and mental health to such a point that they will take huge risks and hunt in the open, during broad daylight, in the same small area, say along a walking trail, where they have encountered pets in order to make a kill." Yet, despite the higher attack statistics, FLNRO doesn't believe Vancouver Island cougars are necessarily more aggressive than those in other locations.

Former Arizona cougar researcher Harley Shaw wondered if being on a relatively isolated island might have something to do with the aggression. Strong ocean currents, plus long distances to other islands or the BC mainland in many areas, could limit dispersal, thus creating a high-density population that must compete for territory and prey. Although some cougars could swim from island to island and possibly reach the mainland, they would likely be a minority.

Dave Eyer speculates that cougars in the relatively isolated gene pool of northern Vancouver Island may be genetically disposed to aggression. As well, poor prey habitat may force young cougars to seek other forms of prey and low prey populations may cause dominant males to increase their territory, thus forcing younger or weaker cougars to find a new range and possibly new prey.

Maurice Hornocker, often referred to as the dean of modern cougar research, agreed that genetics probably plays a role. "We have evidence that some population units are more aggressive than others just like some cities have higher crime rates than others," he said. "I think a genetic link predisposes Vancouver Island mountain lions to aggression. Mountain lions on Vancouver Island and in Idaho, where I conducted most of my research, exhibit extremely different behaviours. It was rare for an Idaho lion to jump from a tree or attack a dog. Yet, when Penny Dewar was studying lions on Vancouver Island, it was a regular occurrence, they almost expected it. That reinforces my personal theory that individual mountain lion populations are predisposed to different behaviours.

"And," he added, "the Vancouver Island cougar population is isolated and heavy hunting pressure over the years quite possibly has selected for aggressive behaviour—aggressive individuals simply survive."

Another possibility is that some cougars may be losing—or never had—a fear of humans. When interviewed in 2004 by Mitchell Gray for a story for *Canadian Geographic,* Bob Hansen, Pacific Rim National Park's wildlife–human conflict specialist at the time, stated, "We know cougars do view people as prey. There is a history of cougars attacking and consuming people. It's a small but ever present risk, and it happens more on Vancouver Island than any other place in North America."

The spring 2011 issue of *Human–Wildlife Interactions* presented another theory about particularly aggressive carnivores. Researchers Dave Mattson, Kenneth Logan and Linda Sweanor pointed out that man-eating carnivores are often specific individuals, prides or packs who attack people in a particular location. They also noted that this activity is learned and can continue for decades. That could explain why wolves often attack humans in Asia and eastern Europe but rarely do so in North America. And why tigers and other big cats in Africa and Asia attack people much more often than cougars attack people in North America. "These behaviours of other species elsewhere in the world serve as a cautionary tale and may partly explain the high concentration of cougar attacks on Vancouver Island," the authors stated near the conclusion of their paper.

If that is so, an in-depth study of Vancouver Island cougars might be able to provide some answers as to what types of stressors may cause clusters of aggression, as well as lead to possible ways of disrupting the behaviour before it's passed on to the next generation.

CHAPTER 12:
Tracking the Elusive Puma

Oh the beautiful, splendid, supple, graceful, powerful,
silent puma! I would rather watch and draw and
dream about it than about any other thing.

—CHARLES LIVINGSTON BULL,
The Century: A Popular Quarterly, 1914

"The hounds were already loose, moving fast on the cougar's fresh scent. The day was cold and clear and the sound of the dogs' excitement filled the air," Penny Dewar recalled in 2012. Back in 1973, she and her husband, Percy, had one rule when it came to winter hunting: never release the hounds after noon. But they'd passed the same spot an hour before and there had been no sign of cougar. Now there were large, round tracks most likely made by an adult male. "How far could he go?" they asked each other. And so the chase was on.

The couple wasn't hunting for bounty or sport. They were conducting the first long-term, in-depth telemetry study of wild cougars in Canada. And they were doing so in the capital of cougar country, Vancouver Island. It all started in 1971 when the BC Fish and Wildlife Branch gave Penny two orphaned cubs. Hoping to replicate studies conducted with African lions, she planned to raise the cougars, release them on Cracroft Island, then follow and observe them. But at three months old the cubs were already too wild to handle, let alone bond with. On December 31, 1971, Penny's future husband, Percy Dewar, knocked on her door. "If you want to learn about cougars, I'll help you," he said.

After the orphaned cougar cubs were placed at a wildlife reserve, Fish and Wildlife suggested the couple radio-collar cougars. Their study area stretched from the Strait of Georgia inland to Mount Arrowsmith and between the Nanaimo and Big Qualicum Rivers. All of their work took place in Percy's guiding territory, most around Northwest Bay in the Englishman River watershed near Parksville. Their goal was to study the population dynamics and behaviour of cougars and determine how many were in the area.

The Dewars were an unlikely duo. When they met, Penny was a petite twenty-three-year-old with a degree in biology. Fifty-two-year-old Percy was extremely strong and fit and had spent most of his life in the bush logging, collecting bounty on cougars and guiding. "But he wasn't just hunting," explained Penny. "He was smart and paid attention to cougar and dog behaviour. Percy's hounds were better trained than most poodles—they never chased deer or anything else, just cougars."

And that's what Lou and Blue were doing late this December 1973 afternoon. Percy ran ahead after the dogs while Penny moved at a slower pace, making notes and taking photographs. "The cougar was travelling," she wrote in an unpublished article titled "Data." "He climbed a high ridge, then down across gullies and through creeks, up another ridge, balanced over icy logs hanging in space, strode over snow and steep rock on and on. I climbed and crawled, slipped and trudged behind.

"Hours passed as well as the light and frail warmth of the sun," she continued. "Wet from snow and effort, I was freezing. I'd lost the trail and Yaka, my Australian shepherd, had lost interest.

Hours more searching, stumbling and cursing, circling and circling until I found an old road. Dark miles further I saw the fire. For thaw and signal, Percy had lit a pitch stump that flared the sky. He too had lost the trail, feared he'd lost me."

With Yaka between them Penny and Percy stood on branches piled at the fire's edge letting the heat melt the frost from their jackets and warm their bodies. "The flames were a wall above and before us," Penny wrote. "We wondered how far the cougar would go before the hounds treed him. We knew they'd bay and bound beneath the tree until their voices died out then collapse in sleep. Once before we'd arrived to find a cougar snoring on a branch and the dogs below opening and shutting their mouths with not a sound coming out. We knew it might be days before we saw them again."

Then something leapt through the flames and Yaka fell through the branches they were standing on. "Suddenly there was a cougar between us," Penny wrote. "Percy and I looked at each other in surprise. The cat looked into our eyes, became frantic and ran."

The Dewars returned the next day to read the story in the snow. When they'd started tracking the cougar they were deep in the woods, far from human habitation. But over the course of the night, they'd travelled to the edge of a neighbourhood—one that the hungry young cougar had staked out as a source of easy prey. "So, while Percy and the hounds chased one cougar, another had followed me and Yaka," explained Penny. "We could see where it had lain on a log at the other side of the fire watching before sailing through the flames. Heedless of me it had stalked my dog and was locked in predator focus. It saw the dog as food and apparently did not notice the humans until it landed between us."

The Dewars studied cougars from 1972 to 1978. For four of those years a 3.5 by 3.5 metre (12 by 12 foot) tent served as headquarters and home. It had cedar shake walls 1.2 metres (4 feet)

Biologist Penny Dewar listens at the telemetry tower outside the tent she shared with her husband, Percy, and up to fifteen dogs at a time while conducting Canada's first long-term, in-depth cougar study in the 1970s.
Photo by Su-San Brown, courtesy Penny Dewar

high, a dirt and plank floor and a tarp roof that "flew when it blew." Amenities included a bed, table and chair set and a bathtub the Dewars had carved out of a cedar log. The tent surrounded a very small travel trailer that served as a storage area, as it was mouse-proof. An airtight stove and a wood cookstove completed the furnishings. At one point the body count in the tent was two humans and fifteen dogs.

Lou, one of Percy's bluetick hounds, was the star of the show. "She never made a mistake, all the dogs deferred to her," said Penny. "We did most of our tracking during the summer. When it's hot and dry scent can dissipate in seconds so we depended on well-trained dogs. Once, a cougar with cubs attacked Lou chewing her up around the head. When she recovered and took over as lead dog again we noticed we weren't treeing any cougars. Percy ran after her one day and discovered that as soon as Lou got close to a cougar she turned back and all the dogs followed her.

"The cougars we encountered seemed to have an instinctive fear of humans," Penny noted. "They'd climb a tree to get away from the dogs but one look at us and they often jumped. They'd leap from fifty or sixty feet up, land on the ground and then leap another thirty or forty feet and start running. They channelled the energy of the initial impact into the next leap."

Even though it was cutting edge at the time, the telemetry equipment of the 1970s was mediocre at best. "If we hadn't lived in the woods and devoted all our time to the research, we wouldn't have learned anything," Penny said. Even so, the Dewars were able to track and document cougar behaviour in a way that had never been done in the Pacific Northwest before. An unexpected discovery was the size of a cougar's range. "Once a female had kittens her area shrunk to about five square miles," said Penny. "Mature males roamed around one thousand square miles. There'd be a central portion within that where they spent most of their time and which they defended as their territory."

The Dewars weren't the first to observe cougars with a scientific eye. In the mid-1930s Frank C. Hibben received a grant from the Southwestern Conservation League in the US to study mountain lions, as the organization feared "this most colorful of American animals was becoming greatly reduced in numbers with little or no knowledge concerning them." So Hibben spent a year hanging out with professional cougar hunters in New Mexico and Arizona. As research for his master's thesis at the University of New Mexico, he studied the big cat's prey, collected scat and talked to ranchers about livestock predation. In addition to his paper, Hibben wrote popular articles for magazines, as well as the book *Hunting American Lions*.

When it comes to cougar research, Maurice Hornocker's work is the cornerstone of knowledge about the big cats. Over the course of his forty-year career, he's studied wildlife worldwide, written books, made documentary films, published more than one hundred scientific articles and served on the board of many wildlife organizations. He also founded the Hornocker Wildlife Institute and later the Selway Institute, a non-profit society dedicated to wildlife research and education.

In the early 1960s Hornocker began the first ever long-term continuous study on mountain lions, pioneered the use of telemetry equipment on the big cats and discovered information that was instrumental in changing the animal's status from vermin to big game species. "At the time, very little research had been conducted on mountain lions," he said. "They're very secretive so difficult to study and there were many misconceptions about them. My idea was to start from scratch, capture and mark all the lions in one location then recapture them over time to study them."

The first winter he tagged and tattooed thirteen lions in western Montana. But the state still had a bounty and nine of his research subjects were killed by spring. So Hornocker shifted his study to an isolated region in the backcountry of Idaho. During the next ten years he captured sixty-four lions three hundred times. This was the first time anyone had really examined the sociology and ecology of the mountain lion and how the animal fit into the environment as predators of deer and elk. A major discovery was that they don't just wander aimlessly but are strongly territorial. Another was that, instead of being a threat to big game, mountain lions kept ungulate populations in check. "Mountain lions have an important place in the environment," Hornocker explained. "Ungulates have the ability to overpopulate and ruin the environment but mountain lions keep the whole system in balance. If the mountain lion population is stable, deer populations in the area will thrive."

Hornocker's groundbreaking research persuaded many western states to reclassify lions as big game, rather than vermin, and thus introduce regulations about hunting them. As public attitudes and the focus of governments shifted, studies on the carnivores increased. And while hounds are still the fastest way to tree a cat, more sophisticated telemetry equipment and the advent of global positioning devices that can document an animal's movements as often as every five minutes have catapulted cougar research into a new era. Velcro is strategically placed to obtain fur samples, trail cameras record previously unknown journeys and DNA obtained from fur, scat or blood has the potential to identify individual cougars no matter what geographical or political boundaries they cross.

So what do we now know about cougars? More than ever before, but just enough to raise additional questions. The truth is no one even knows how many cougars live in any state or province, let alone in North and South America as a whole. But ongoing field-work continues to provide new information about the predator's behaviour as well as insights into cougar–human dynamics.

Witnessing a flock of sandhill cranes fly overhead one day while she was treeplanting in a remote BC location convinced Danielle Thompson that she wanted to learn more about wildlife and their habitats to ensure their continued presence on the landscape. Soon afterwards, she enrolled in the wildlife management program of the University of Northern BC. Now she's a resource management and public safety specialist at the Long Beach Unit of Pacific Rim National Park Reserve.

In the mid-2000s research projects in the park examined the habitat needs of cougars, the impact of increasing visitor numbers and social reactions to large carnivores. As part of the WildCoast Project, Thompson analysed West Coast Trail visitor data and human–cougar interaction data from 1993 to 2006. "It's hard to determine if people were seeing the same cat or different ones," she said. "We know that in 2005 some siblings' home range overlapped the West Coast Trail and that they had multiple interactions with different people. So there aren't necessarily more cougars just because more activity is noticed."

Thompson observed that cougar sightings on the West Coast Trail appeared to be cyclical with peaks of activity occurring every two to three years. It's suspected this cycle may relate to the availability of larger-sized prey, such as deer, and competition with local wolf populations for prey. "What the research did show, however," she said, "was that the majority of human–cougar encounters occurred during times when human use levels were low. This indicates that cougars are trying to avoid interactions with people."

Students from the University of Alberta began studying cougars in the Central East Slopes and Cypress Hills regions of the province in 2004 and 2007. "There hadn't been any cougars in the Cypress Hills for a hundred years," noted Mark Boyce, professor and Alberta Conservation Association Chair in Fisheries and Wildlife at the University of Alberta. "Ranchers were anxious and angry as they were convinced they were losing livestock to cougars. At times they were so hostile I wondered if the student conducting the study could handle the pressure. The ranchers were also making accusations that Alberta Parks was releasing cougars into the area.

"That wasn't the case at all," Boyce continued. "The cougars were travelling up the coulees and Red Deer River Valley from the mountains in the west to repopulate their former range. But what was surprising was that out of the three hundred and fifty to four hundred cougar kills that took place during the study, not one was livestock. If an animal dies of disease or natural causes and is scavenged by coyotes some people will think it was killed by a cougar. But if you know what to look for and get to the carcass soon enough, it's easy to tell if a cougar was responsible. The student conducting the study examined every cougar kill during the study and not one was livestock."

Farther south, the Teton Cougar Project, based out of Jackson Hole, Wyoming, is examining the predator–prey relationships and demographics of cougars in the region, as well as how they're adapting to the expansion of wolves and grizzly bears into their habitat. "We want to know everything about these cougars: what they eat, how they relate to each other and how wolves and grizzlies are affecting their lives and populations," said Howard Quigley, the Teton Cougar Project director and executive director of jaguar programs at Panthera, the world's leading cat conservation organization.

Quigley became involved with cougars in a roundabout way. While working with bears in Tennessee, he was invited to study pandas in China then jaguars in Brazil. He met Maurice Hornocker

Maurice Hornocker's groundbreaking research in the wilderness of central Idaho during the 1960s was a major influence in the reclassification of mountain lions from bounty hunted vermin to big game species. In this photo he's holding a forty-pound (eighteen-kilogram) cub that, along with its entire family, was tagged and tattooed as part of the study. *Photo courtesy Maurice Hornocker*

Advanced technology, such as the telemetry equipment being used by Howard Quigley, director of the Teton Cougar Project in Wyoming, allows researchers to better understand the movements and behaviour of cougars. *Photo by Brad Boner, courtesy Panthera*

while completing his doctorate at the University of Idaho, eventually becoming president of the Hornocker Wildlife Institute and working on long-term cougar projects in Idaho, New Mexico, Yellowstone National Park and now even parts of Latin America, where jaguars and cougars coexist.

"Technology has opened up a whole new world of studies," he said. "Before we could only obtain DNA if we took a sample of blood from an animal. Now there are several ways to fingerprint individuals and determine who they're related to, it's very exciting. And GPS radio collars and high-definition trail cameras allow us to capture behavior that has never been seen before."

Quigley recently watched a video of a male and a female cougar at an elk kill suddenly crouching, looking off camera and then running away. Shortly afterward, a big wolf appeared on the film. On another occasion, the Teton team discovered that F1, the female cougar profiled in the National Geographic video *American Cougar*, had lost two of her three kittens to a wolf pack. "Cougars adjusting to other large carnivores in the environment hasn't really been studied in this detail before," said Quigley. "It's a rare opportunity in the field of science to witness these changes."

Initially partnered with Craighead Beringia South, a wildlife research and education institute, the Teton Cougar Project began in 2001 and Quigley hopes it will continue through 2015 or even 2017. "With its collage of federal and private multi-use lands and protected areas, as well as amenities such as an airport, major highway and town, Jackson Hole is an ideal location for a long-term study like this," he commented. "There aren't many places where you can roll out of bed and be at the site of a cougar kill within forty minutes. It's this type of long-term, intensive fieldwork that's necessary to get the information we're obtaining."

The program's proximity to wilderness resulted in Quigley becoming the first wildlife biologist to witness and report on a wild cougar adoption. After a hunter killed a female cougar with three young cubs in 2007, another female cougar, also with three kittens, adopted the orphans. Quigley believes the adopting female was the adult daughter of the dead cougar. "This kind of altruism is seen in many animals, including birds and humans, and is usually limited to those with close relations," he wrote in an article for Panthera.

Another revelation occurred one winter day in 2012 when Teton team member Drew Rush went looking for F51. Following the vHF signal from her collar, he found the female and her two kittens. But he also saw two other cubs and another adult female cougar that weren't collared. Then to top it off, a male cougar arrived and all seven of the big cats fed off the same kill. This was a shocker as it's generally believed cougars are solitary animals, never travelling or eating together unless it's a mother and cubs, young siblings recently out on their own or a mating pair.

This gathering of cougars raises interesting questions about how, when and why they might socialize with each other. And it turns out the 2012 meet-up wasn't an isolated event. In their Vancouver Island study the Dewars radio tracked a get-together between two adult cougars that they suspected were mother and daughter. "They spent about thirty minutes together," said Penny. "And what was interesting, was that they both had kittens but left them behind."

And when Brad Thomas set up a motion-sensor camera on a trail near Wenatchee, Washington, in February 2011, he got more than he bargained for. Thomas had never seen a cougar in the wild but his camera recorded a gathering of eight of them. Wildlife biologists examined the photo and declared it legit. Because mother and daughter cougars sometimes have close or even overlapping ranges, they speculated that it was a mother and her adult daughter, both with kittens. One of the biologists recalled seeing a 1960s photo of seven cougars crossing a bridge over the Stehekin River, also in Washington state.

As it turns out, cougars are full of surprises. During the bounty years poisoned bait was often used to exterminate wolves but wasn't considered effective for cougars as they weren't scavengers. But the research team at the UC Davis Wildlife Health Center has experienced incredible success using dead deer as bait for mountain lions. In 2001 a cougar even stole a dead deer out of their pickup. "I learned several lessons from that," said Walter Boyce, wildlife veterinarian and professor at UC Davis. "The puma found the deer by smell, not sight; he wasn't fazed by the streetlight and unnatural touch and smell of the truck and he ate and cached the carcass, treating the deer just as he would one he had killed himself."

Between January 2001 and October 2003, the UC Davis team placed forty-four deer carcasses at twenty-three locations to study puma scavenging. Eight to twelve pumas scavenged at nearly half of the spots and some—ranging in age from eleven months to nine years—were captured seven times at scavenging sites. They took carcasses that were frozen, fresh or rotten. And all, except tethered carcasses, were treated as if it was the cougar's own kill. One radio-collared puma frequently scavenged carcasses from a domestic livestock graveyard.

In 2005, the UC Davis team were radio collaring lions in the Santa Ana Mountains. They set a trap and a cat went in and tripped the door release within an hour. Boyce and the others were eating dinner at a cabin located in the Santa Rosa Plateau Ecological Reserve half a kilometre (a quarter of a mile) away when the radio transmitter went off. When they checked the cage thirty minutes later they found a healthy, twenty-six-kilogram (fifty-seven-pound) male lion about a year old. While they waited for the tranquilizer dart to take effect, Eric York checked the videotape from the motion-sensor camera they'd set up outside the cage.

It showed the lion approach and enter the trap, then pace back and forth and peer between the wires. "Suddenly, another set of eyes glowed in the darkness, and a second puma emerged," said Boyce. "This puma clawed and dug at the back of the cage and we wondered, was he trying to get the trapped puma out, or did he want the deer?"

The lion circled the trap and jumped onto a large overhanging oak limb. Then a third, much larger lion appeared. As the team realized that there were at least three mountain lions, most likely a mother and cubs, in the area and only one was in the trap, they became more attuned to the darkness around them. Before moving the drugged lion closer to the cabin to examine him, they reset the trap. Forty-five minutes later the door clanged shut. The second young lion was in the trap. They repeated their health check, attached a radio collar and called it a night. Two evenings later, using another frozen deer, they caught the six-year-old mother mountain lion at the same location. And six months later they recaptured all three lions within a few days employing the same method.

"We now know this behaviour is not unusual," said Boyce. "Pumas are predators *and* scavengers. Hunting and killing your dinner is hard work. And there is always the risk of being injured by your prey. A puma whose nose leads it to a dead deer finds an easy meal. The difficult part of capturing cougars this way is obtaining bait, it's labour intensive. We work closely with agencies that monitor road networks. When we get a call about a deer carcass on the road someone goes out to pick it up."

Finding dead deer to use as bait is one thing, but discovering wildlife where you don't expect it is another. Some terrestrial mammals in North America are amazing scientists with their long walkabouts. In 2008, DNA from fur and feces revealed that a wolverine in the Sierra Nevada Mountains of northeast California had travelled approximately a thousand kilometres (six hundred miles) from the Sawtooth Mountains in Idaho. A radio-collared fisher, also from Idaho, surprised researchers by regularly meandering sixty-nine kilometres (forty-three miles), a remarkable feat for such a small animal. Gray wolves are also wandering back to Wisconsin, and coyotes are creeping eastward.

Cougars are getting into the act too. When they're about eighteen months to two years old their mother lets them know it's time to be independent. Besides honing their hunting skills, they

Howard Quigley and field staff examine a cougar and record data such as weight, length and general health as part of the Teton Cougar Project in Wyoming. *Photos by Steve Winter, courtesy Panthera*

also have to find and claim their own home turf. According to *Cougar: Ecology and Conservation*, edited by Maurice Hornocker and Sharon Negri, a male cougar's territory may range from 120 to 1,125 square kilometres (75 to 700 square miles) depending on habitat and prey. A female's will typically be around 40 to 80 square kilometres (25 to 50 square miles). Male ranges overlap with female ranges and sometimes those of other males, although the males tend to avoid each other.

Dispersing is necessary to control cougar populations and to prevent inbreeding. But the search for home ground is a perilous journey. Young cougars are at increased risk of death due to starvation, close contact with humans or being hit by vehicles. It's especially dangerous for young males who are chased out of other males' territories and are sometimes—perhaps often—killed in the process. Female cougars seem more tolerant when it comes to sharing their territory. Many adolescent females establish ranges within a five-minute walk of mom's, and may even overlap it.

Cougars require habitat that provides enough cover for stalking, along with adequate prey. And, as well as needing to find a spot that's not occupied by a dominant tom, young males need mates. In a 2010 South Dakota State University paper titled "Dispersal Movements of Subadult Cougars from the Black Hills," Daniel J. Thompson and Jonathon A. Jenks noted that even if a territory is vacant and adequate prey is present, a male cougar tends to continue travelling until he finds those conditions plus one or more available females.

It's normal for a young male to disperse 160 to 480 kilometres (100 to 300 miles), but apparently some are prepared to walk even farther in their search for sex. In 2004 scientists were astonished when a young adult male cougar weighing 52 kilograms (114 pounds) was killed by a train near Red Rock, Oklahoma. Its

Winston Vickers of the UC Davis Wildlife Heath Center prepares to dart a mountain lion as another team member distracts it. Unlike most researchers, the UC Davis team doesn't use hounds to tree their subjects. Instead they bait traps to capture lions. And since the big cats are most active during the darker hours, the field crew often works the night shift. *Photo by Pablo Bryant, courtesy UC Davis Wildlife Health Centre*

radio collar identified it as part of a South Dakota University research project in the Black Hills of South Dakota. Experts figure that in the eleven months since the cougar was tagged, it travelled at least 1,600 kilometres (1,000 miles). Four years later, DNA from a young adult cougar shot in Chicago (the first recorded in the city since 1855) suggested he also hailed from the Black Hills and had covered around the same distance.

But who would expect to find a wild cougar a ninety-minute drive from New York City? Especially when the last documented sighting in the state was in the late 1800s. Apparently Paul Beier, a cougar researcher, professor at Northern Arizona University and president of the Society for Conservation Biology, did. When asked how far he thought migrating cougars might go, he speculated they would reach New Jersey. And when an SUV hit a young adult male outside Milford, Connecticut, in June 2011, he was proved right. The healthy 64-kilogram (140-pound) cat was collared in the Black Hills in 2009. By the time he met his death two years later, it's estimated he walked 2,415 to 2,900 kilometres (1,500 to 1,800 miles)—the longest recorded journey of any North American land mammal to date. In an ironic twist of fate, the cougar was run over just three months after the U.S. Fish and Wildlife Service declared the eastern cougar extinct.

But what's more significant is that male mountain lions aren't the only ones travelling long distances. Since 1996, Utah State University has been studying lions in the Monroe and Oquirrh mountain ranges. Now in its seventeenth year, it's one of the longest continuously comparative lion studies in the world. In February 2005, researchers fitted a young female cougar in the Oquirrh Mountains with a GPS radio collar. She was only 354 kilometres (220 miles) away when a hunter shot her in Meeker, Colorado, a year later. But her GPS unit revealed she'd travelled more than 1,340 kilometres (833 miles), crossing an interstate highway and three major rivers, as well as climbing a 3,350-metre (11,000-foot) mountain along the way. Three years later, a young female cougar killed in Saskatoon was found wearing a collar from the Black Hills study. It's estimated she'd travelled more than 1,100 kilometres (684 miles). And in March 2013, a mature female cougar, also from the Black Hills, was killed 676 kilometres (420 miles) away in Montana.

What's particularly interesting about these incredible journeys is that five out of the six cats originated in the Black Hills, where mountain lions became locally extinct in the early 1900s. Over

SOME CONFIRMED COUGAR SIGHTINGS OUTSIDE OF ESTABLISHED RANGE

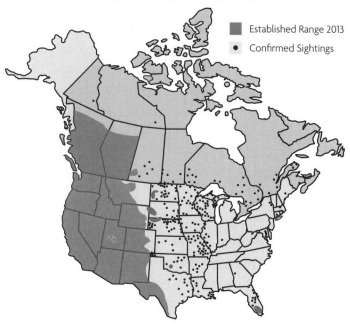

Dots indicate confirmed sightings as cougars migrate out of established range. *Information from the Cougar Network, Government of Canada agencies and François-Joseph Lapointe of the Université de Montréal*

time, they recolonized the area on their own and estimates of the population in 2010 ranged from 150 to 300 animals. Although the majority of cougars dispersing long distances have been young adult males, the fact that some females are doing so—plus increased documented sightings in the Midwest and southern and eastern Canada and the US—indicates the possibility of additional colonies being established.

Who knows? Perhaps cougars will eventually reclaim their former habitat and roam North America from coast to coast. But will people residing in areas that haven't had cougar populations for more than a century be prepared to accept the predator?

CHAPTER 13:
Sharing the Landscape

Each of our native wild creatures is in itself a
precious heritage that we have no right to destroy
or put beyond the reach of our children.

—ERNEST THOMPSON SETON, *Lives of the Hunted*

As Erin Laberge was riding her bike through the East Wellington area of Nanaimo on Vancouver Island, she noticed a golden retriever in the ditch. A car was coming the other way so she pedalled toward the dog to prevent it from running onto the road. But as she passed, she realized it wasn't a dog, it was a cougar. The eighteen-year-old skidded to a stop, then her flight instinct kicked in. Leaning over the handlebars she pumped her legs as hard as she could, convinced she could outrun the cat.

But the cougar followed, coming within seven metres (twenty-two feet). "You know how you have a bad dream and you're running away from something and your legs are shaking? It was like that," she told Chris Bush, a reporter for the *Nanaimo News Bulletin*. Then Laberge recalled what she'd learned at school and from her parents. She stopped, placed her bike in front of her and began yelling and ringing her bike bell. The cougar froze, then just watched as Laberge rode to a nearby elementary school where she called her dad and asked him to pick her up.

Laberge's family lives on a rural property and she'd seen cougars before, but this was the first time one had acted aggressively. "You kind of lose your common sense when you're scared...that's why I started to bike away so fast," she told Bush. "It's a good thing I remembered my training or it could have been a lot worse."

Laberge's encounter is an excellent example of how understanding predatory behaviour can prevent an encounter from escalating into an attack. That type of knowledge is exactly what's needed for humans and cougars to share the landscape with the least amount of risk to both. And that's important because, in addition to being a symbol of all that is beautiful, wild and free, cougars are also an essential component of a healthy environment.

"Cougars are an important wilderness icon and big game species in their own right," said Mark Boyce of the University of Alberta. "Biologists are increasingly emphasizing the importance of predation by large carnivores in structuring ecosystems. Great care must be made to manage this low-density, wide-ranging predator."

Cougars are a keystone species, and healthy cougar populations play a vital role in the delicate balance of ecological communities. They cull animals that are old, diseased or weak and their presence prevents ungulates from overgrazing. Cougars also help control smaller mammal populations, and the remains of their kills contribute to the food chain of birds, insects and other animals. Even the decomposition of their prey provides nutrients for the soil. Remove cougars from the ecological equation and over time the dynamics between wildlife and the environment can change dramatically.

"We now have overwhelming evidence that large predators are hugely important in the function of nature, from the deepest oceans to the highest mountains, the tropics and the Arctic," said William Ripple. A professor of forestry at Oregon State University and director of its Trophic Cascades Program, Ripple co-authored a report compiling the findings of twenty-four international scientists regarding the decline and destruction of predators worldwide. "The effect is much greater than we thought," he explained. "It contributes to pollution, loss of habitat, climate change, invasive species and the spread of disease. These predators and processes ultimately protect humans. This isn't just about them, it's about us."

Conservation and management of a species is often a contentious issue involving personal beliefs, public perception and government regulations. Mention the M-word to carnivore experts, big cat organizations and government officials and the reaction is similar to tossing a handful of feed pellets into a tank of hungry fish. There's a frenzy of opinion but consensus is rare. Some say cougar numbers are increasing; others are adamant they're on the decline. Various groups advocate controlled hunting; others say it should be banned altogether. And hunting with hounds is a debate all on its own. Many experts consider large chunks of habitat linked by generous dispersal corridors mandatory, while others are convinced dispersal corridors nine metres (thirty feet) wide with plenty of cover are adequate. And each of those beliefs may be correct for different cougar populations in different regions at different times.

The International Union for Conservation of Nature currently lists the puma as a species of least concern with an estimated population of around 50,000. Although some studies have been conducted in Central and South America, information on the big cats in these areas is generally scarce. Some countries protect them while others allow extensive hunting. "Pumas are very adaptable," noted

As large predators, cougars are a vital component of the environments they inhabit.

Howard Quigley, who in his position as executive director of jaguar programs at Panthera visits Latin America regularly. "I've seen puma paw prints from the alpine to the Amazon, and in southern Brazil and Bolivia populations are strong. But, like jaguars, they get into trouble with livestock. And they don't tend to be that populous in densely forested areas like the Amazon. They thrive in more open habitat and those are usually the first areas that are developed for agriculture and ranching. So there have been some conflicts and losses."

As is the case in countries south of the US, cougar management in Canada and the US varies with each state and province. In the eastern portion of the continent, Florida is home to the only known breeding population east of the Mississippi. In 1967, when their numbers plummeted to less than thirty cats, they were classified as endangered. By the 1980s signs of inbreeding such as kinked tails, cowlicks, heart defects and an inclination toward parasites were evident. Most males had abnormal sperm and one or both of their testicles had failed to descend.

To preserve the population, eight females were imported from Texas. Three died but the rest successfully bred and produced litters free from genetic abnormalities. According to information provided by Ken Warren, a public affairs officer with the U.S. Fish and Wildlife Service in southern Florida, there are approximately 100 to 160 adult and sub-adult panthers in the southwestern part of the state. Some males have migrated north of the Caloosahatchee River to establish their own territories, too. In 2000, one almost made it to Disney World, thirty-four kilometres (twenty-one miles) southwest of Orlando, before his radio-collar transmitter failed, leaving researchers unsure of his fate. Hopes are high that some females will follow the males' migration route to form a breeding colony but none have been documented north of the river since 1973.

Being hit by vehicles and intraspecies fighting are the major causes of death for Florida panthers. And although there are several public areas that provide good habitat, such as Big Cypress National Preserve, Everglades National Park and the Florida

Panther National Wildlife Refuge, the population needs more space if it is to remain genetically diverse and continue to increase. In 2012, the Everglades Headwaters National Wildlife Refuge and Conservation Area was established to provide habitat for panthers moving north. And a 570-hectare (1,400-acre) area known as the Panther Dispersal Zone was secured to maintain a natural migration corridor.

Cougar (*Puma concolor*)
- Historic Range
- Current Range

Information from Panthera

California, which has banned sports hunting since 1990, is the only other state to protect the big cat to such a degree. Although Marc Kenyon of the California Department of Fish and Wildlife estimates mountain lion numbers at four thousand and dropping, some residents believe the population has peaked and hunting should be reintroduced. In southern portions of the state, an increasing human population and the resulting development threatens lion habitat and has fragmented dispersal corridors. And freeways are a major cause of mortality, as they are in Florida. "Even when an underpass is built for wildlife, we've seen lions go right up to it, then cross the road and get killed," said Winston Vickers of the UC Davis Wildlife Health Center.

Aside from Florida and California, where hunting is banned, the other dozen or so states with confirmed breeding populations of mountain lions control hunting to some extent. Regulations are perhaps the most relaxed in Texas where lions of any age and sex can be hunted and trapped in any numbers at any time of year as long as a person has a hunting licence. Jonah Evans, a wildlife diversity biologist for the Trans Pecos Region of the Texas Parks and Wildlife Department, said the Lone Star state currently has two primary populations of lions. There are no official estimates as to numbers, but the lion population in the western portion of the state is considered healthy while the one in the south is thought to have declined by more than fifty percent. Evans speculated that the reduced numbers are the result of the mountain lions being isolated from other source populations in western Texas and Mexico, combined with habitat loss and possibly overhunting.

The majority of cougar populations in the western states and provinces are considered healthy and stable. In British Columbia, the cat is classed as a big game species and, as of 2013, the Ministry of Forests, Lands and Natural Resource Operations estimated

As of 2013, Florida is the only location east of the Mississippi with a confirmed breeding population of pumas. "Protect the Panther" license plates raise awareness about the felines and fund conservation efforts. *Courtesy Florida Fish and Wildlife Conservation Commission*

there are 5,100 to 7,000 cougars in the province. Around 600 of them reside on Vancouver Island, an increase of about fifty percent from previous years. In email correspondence, FLNRO stated, "British Columbia is home to the largest and most intact cougar population of any jurisdiction in North America and they play an important functional role in the ecosystem." It was therefore a surprise to find out the province has no cougar management plan other than a preliminary draft dating back to 1980. Granted, unless there are conservation concerns, most species don't have management plans. Cougars are, however, regulated through CITES (Convention on the International Trade in Endangered Species) as an Appendix II species for which trade is permitted but may need to be regulated, so the province is obligated to develop an updated management plan. It's been in the works since 2011, or perhaps longer, but as of December 2012 government officials were unable to provide a target completion date.

Like BC, Alberta has a healthy cougar population and regulates hunting. The province has approximately two thousand cougars and is in the process of updating its 1992 management plan. Saskatchewan, with an estimated three to four hundred cougars, is the site of Canada's most eastern breeding population, which is located in the Cypress Hills. As for the rest of Canada, the big cats have been sighted as far north as the Yukon and Northwest Territories and as far east as New Brunswick and Nova Scotia. Small populations have been confirmed in Ontario and Quebec but no one knows if they're breeding. The federal Committee on the Status of Endangered Wildlife in Canada says there is insufficient data to assess the animal's status in eastern provinces.

Some eastern states and provinces boast that they've never had a human fatality from a cougar attack. No doubt that's true for the last one hundred years or so, as cougars were extirpated in the last century. But evidence that the big cats are migrating east means governments may need to develop cougar management plans in the future. And more importantly, ensure residents and visitors know the appropriate way to respond if they encounter one of the big cats.

Due to their secretive nature, it's difficult to determine how many cougars are in any given region, never mind the age, sex and condition of the animals, or prey availability and other considerations necessary for a healthy population. "The main challenge is the same today as when I tracked mountain lions in the seventies," said Harley Shaw, a former research biologist with the Arizona Game and Fish Department. "We're still discovering information about the detailed behaviour of this elusive animal. Mountain lions are so difficult to observe, we've just scratched the surface of what their day-to-day behaviour is."

A recently completed thirteen-year Washington State University (WSU) research project provided some fresh insights into cougar ecology. And the information was significant enough to convince the Washington Department of Fish and Wildlife to implement a new cougar management plan as of January 2013. It turns out old toms are a stabilizing influence. They're experienced hunters and usually avoid humans. For obvious reasons, though, they're the animals trophy hunters seek out. Every time a mature male is shot, one or more young males move into the now vacant territory. And these cats are the ones that often get into trouble with humans. Mature males also regulate how many young males are in the area by chasing them out of their range or killing them. The study, lead by Rob Wielgus, director of WSU's Large Carnivore Conservation Lab, revealed that overharvesting mature male cougars allows more young males to survive, thus increasing the potential for negative encounters between predators and humans, livestock and game. So an increase in human–cougar altercations might be due to the ages of the animals, not their numbers. Washington's new equilibrium management plan limits the number of cougars harvested in an effort to retain a more natural age range in the state's cougar population.

Many studies have taken place since Maurice Hornocker first started radio collaring cougars in the 1960s. But each one only provides a piece of the puzzle that is the puma. An article written by Kyle and Aliah Knopff and Michelle Bacon titled "North of 49: Ongoing Cougar Research in Alberta" noted, "Despite this relative abundance of information there is still much to be learned about these fascinating predators. This is especially true in Canada, where, with a few important exceptions (e.g. the excellent 10-year Southern Alberta study conducted by Orval Pall, Ian Ross, and Martin Jalkotzy in the 1980s and early 1990s), a comparatively small portion of all the cougar research in North America has been undertaken."

Which brings up a good question. Why is Canada the site of so few long-term, in-depth field studies? Especially British

Columbia, which has the largest cougar population in North America, as well as the highest rate of attacks and fatalities. Perhaps funding is more available and generous in the United States, or maybe it's because that country has more academic wildlife programs. Maurice Hornocker pointed out that there is a wider variety of cougar habitat in the US and that different state fish and game and conservation departments are pressured by constituents to find out if cougars are killing too many deer. "And where you have more people and more cougars sharing the same habitat," he added, "such as in the suburbs of Colorado and California, that creates more of a demand for studies."

"Long-term studies are absolutely necessary," said Howard Quigley, the project director for the Teton Cougar Project in Jackson Hole, Wyoming, which began in 2001. "A typical wildlife species study lasts three to five years. If we'd quit within that time period, we wouldn't have been able to pose and answer so many questions. And the more we know, the more we understand what is needed for cougar conservation."

In addition to more long-term studies and the funding to support them, information needs to be (and to some degree already is) freely shared by agencies in different regions—as cougars don't recognize state, provincial and national borders. Ken Logan and Linda Sweanor, who have studied mountain lions for decades in numerous locations, including an intensive ten-year project in New Mexico, advocate management zones. These would be based on geographic terrain and habitat rather than political boundaries. Zones could include regions for sports hunting, controlled killing in regions with high human or livestock populations, and dedicated refuges for mountain lions and other wildlife where needed. As yet, no state or province has opted to explore this innovative concept.

A valuable tool would be a North American DNA database that could be utilized to track cougars as they move from one jurisdiction to another. Standardized forms for recording information about encounters, attacks and fatalities that included information on the age, sex and condition of each cougar, as well as what the cougar and human(s) were doing before and during the incident, would aid researchers searching for commonalities among these events and provide further insight into the behaviour of cougars.

South Dakota has an efficient way of collecting information on its mountain lion population. All lions shot during hunting season must be taken to the state's Game, Fish and Parks Commission, where biologists measure and weigh the animal, take tissue and tooth samples, and record information regarding sex, age, general health and injuries. After a hunter removes the head, pelt and any edible portions they want, most carcasses are sent to South Dakota State University for a full necropsy.

The leading causes of death for wild pumas are disease and being killed by another cougar. But humans affect the lives of the big cats too and research in southern California indicates that humans and the resulting development are a major threat to the sustainability of some lion populations. Public attitude drives conservation and determines how governments manage large carnivores and respond to altercations. But no matter how rare encounters are, just saying the word "cougar" or "mountain lion" generates strong emotions, ranging from overwhelming fear to absolute awe.

Today, if a cougar is shot after it attacks or kills someone, there's often a negative reaction from the public. Typical comments in letters to the editor include, "Don't shoot cougars, we're in their territory." "If someone is in cougar territory and gets attacked, too bad, it's their fault!" "I never report a cougar or bear sighting as I know the authorities will just shoot it." Conservation officers and mayors have received threatening phone calls and letters after problem cougars have been put down. And cougar hunters and guides have found razor blades in letters and their dogs have been threatened. In the movie *Bambi*, wild animals are clearly the good guys and humans the bad guys. But in real life there are dangerous people and dangerous cougars.

"When it comes to cougars, our society has some extreme protectionists and some extreme exploiters," stated Maurice Hornocker. "Somewhere in the middle is the answer. I always advise that when a cougar is habituated and in areas close to humans where there is a potential threat, it should be humanely removed. If possible, that means tranquillizing and releasing it in the wilderness. If that's not possible, the cat should be humanely euthanized with no apologies made. In North America thousands of dogs and cats are euthanized each year. An attack on a child does much more harm to the cougar's reputation than removing one bad individual."

Following David Parker's attack on Vancouver Island, an online commenter asked, "Did he really have to kill the cougar?" The answer is obvious. It was either kill the cougar or be killed. And if Parker did somehow manage to escape without killing or seriously injuring the cougar, the possibility that it would attack someone else is high. If a cougar attacks a person it's usually young, old, sick or starving, all conditions that would likely make it desperate enough to try again. Or it has begun to see humans as prey, a view that wouldn't change due to a failed kill. As one woman who asked to remain anonymous commented, "People have lost touch with the reality of wildlife." Wild animals are inherently unpredictable and sometimes dangerous. Cougars are highly evolved killing machines and if they turn that energy toward people, human life must be paramount.

That's often where the decision to shoot a cougar with a tranquillizing dart or a bullet comes in. Depending on the animal's size, physical condition and the amount of adrenaline coursing through its body, a tranquillizer can take anywhere from five to thirty minutes to render the cat unconscious. That lag time can be a problem if the cat is treed in a neighbourhood or cornered in the bushes at a shopping mall and a lot of people are around. Having a mad, scared and half-doped-up carnivore on the loose for even a short time is a very high-risk situation. And if a cougar is tranquillized, the options are to euthanize it later, take it to a zoo or relocate it. Quietly euthanizing it later might save some bad publicity in the short term but the zoo option is usually a no-go unless the cougar is very young. And relocating cougars is tricky. Wildlife conflict manager Mike Badry, who is with the Conservation Officer Service of the BC Ministry of Environment, said, "Very few cougars are suitable for capture and release. If the cougar is considered a risk to public safety or verified as preying on livestock, it will be killed. If a cougar is in an urban area but has not acted aggressively toward people or pets, and there is an opportunity to safely capture the animal, it is a candidate for release back into a wilderness area."

But there's no guarantee relocation will work. Cougars are highly territorial, so if one is dumped in another's range, chances are it will be chased out. Or there may be a fight between the resident cat and the interloper, resulting in serious injury or death. Some relocated cougars end up right back where they came from. "Most research indicates that relocated mountain lions just bounce around from one home range to another being kicked around by resident lions until they find a clear spot," said Marc Kenyon, the black bear, mountain lion and wild pig programs coordinator for the state of California. "They get real beat up along the way, which isn't good as it often results in a dead lion. If we move a lion that's causing a problem in California, we're just moving the problem from one person's backyard to another's."

On June 30, 2011, two cougars around eighteen months old were caught and radio collared near Banff National Park, a prime tourist destination in the Rocky Mountains west of Calgary, Alberta. Their mother had been killed and the orphans were following people. As they seemed healthy and curious rather than aggressive, officials decided to move them into the wilderness near Canmore, Alberta. Two weeks later one attacked a dog and cornered three mountain bikers. When the cat refused to leave, even after being pelted with rocks, the bikers called for help on a cellphone. They had to be escorted out of the vicinity by armed RCMP officers. When the cougar was shot, it was obvious that it hadn't been able to fend for itself and was starving. A couple of weeks later its sibling, also in poor condition, was killed after injuring a six-year-old girl in nearby Bow Valley Provincial Park.

Beginning in August the same year, Squamish, BC, experienced a spike in cougar sightings. Like most of the province, the Squamish area is great cougar country and has experienced aggressive cougars in the past. What was described as a "large, healthy cougar" stalked and approached three groups of mountain bikers in one day near Alice Lake despite their yelling and throwing rocks. Trails were closed but the cougar wasn't found. By September the community, which averages 40 to 60 cougar sightings per year, had recorded 145.

The evening of September 9, Jim Sandford was closing the back door of his house when he noticed a cougar's tail less than a metre (two feet) away on the deck. He looked toward the trees at the rear of his Garibaldi Heights property to find another cougar staring at him. The forty-six-year-old had lived in Squamish for twenty years and he'd never seen a cougar until he spotted these two playing with one of his shoes outside the house the week before. Sandford hadn't reported that sighting but told a reporter, "When they came back...it sealed their fate." Conservation officers killed the young adult cougars around 8:30 that night. As well as being suspects in the stalking of the cyclists, they were becoming increasingly bold around people and had killed at least one house cat.

That night, around 3:45 a.m., the sound of a chirping bird woke Sandford up. The noise would come closer then move away. Curious, he got up and aimed a flashlight outside. That's when he realized the chirping was the mother cougar looking for her cubs. She too was killed by conservation officers.

Even though it was obvious the cougars weren't good candidates for relocation, letters to the editor included comments such as "Killing three cougars is criminal" and "Why kill cougars for just hanging around?" Sandford's take on the situation, however, was solidly based in reality. "We chose to live at the edge of the forest," he said in an interview with *The Province*. "If I step back there, I'm prey. If people don't like that, they can move to a condo in downtown Vancouver."

That's where cougar management really starts, with each individual who lives, works or visits cougar country assuming responsibility for the safety of themselves as well as their children, pets and livestock. And a big part of that involves not inviting predators into communities. "People are very tolerant of deer," said Danielle Thompson of the Pacific Rim National Park Reserve. "Deer attract large predators; you can't really have one without the other. By being tolerant of deer we're sending a positive signal to cougars and wolves that our backyard is a good source of food."

Deer come into towns and yards to munch on grass, flowers and hedges and the generous handouts some people provide even though it's illegal to feed wildlife. Community newspapers often run photos from readers showing deer eating, napping and even giving birth in their yards. Wild deer normally do most of their grazing at dawn, dusk and throughout the night, which is also prime dining time for cougars. But in an urban environment, deer quickly learn that people aren't a threat and become active during the day. Allowing deer to loiter in yards and communities disrupts their natural feeding patterns and can increase the risk of predators making daytime forays into human use areas. Other small mammals such as raccoons have also adapted well to civilization and are found in many cities. They too have the potential to attract predators.

People enjoy watching wildlife and even purchase homes in locations where they can do so. A Washington state study revealed that most people are not motivated to deter wildlife until they or someone in their neighbourhood has a negative encounter. Even when predators such as cougars are near homes, they aren't always discouraged. There's more than one YouTube video online showing a family watching a cougar on their deck as it eyes their pet and paws at the sliding glass door. One family in Boulder, Colorado, even invited neighbours over to watch a mountain lion and its two cubs feed on a deer it had killed in their backyard. The only problem was, once the deer was eaten, mama lion started stalking the mom of the house.

The thrill of witnessing seldom-seen wildlife from the perceived safety of a house is hard to resist. But not making noise and scaring the animal off is the same as setting out a welcome mat for carnivores. They soon learn that approaching buildings and humans poses no danger and they may eventually decide humans look like easy prey. The same dynamics come into play if a cougar is seen in the wild and doesn't immediately run away. Pausing to take photos before aggressively responding to an animal's presence may convince it to investigate humans more thoroughly, if not this time, perhaps the next. It's also important to report cougars that don't flee from humans or that act curious or aggressive as soon as possible, so wildlife officials can track potential problem animals, post warnings at trailheads and alert the public. Reporting sightings also provides an opportunity to attempt to deter the cats with aversive techniques and/or relocate young cougars if possible. But convincing cougars they can't hang around has to happen before they become habituated.

Cougars range over large territories so if one is seen, it might just be passing by. But if it has an uncomfortable experience, it may decide to avoid buildings and other signs of people altogether in the future. Wildlife officials sometimes use rubber bullets to scare them off and residents might want to try bear bangers or the loud clanging of pots and pans from an open window. The blast of an air horn or whistle might also persuade a cougar to move along. For rural residents with more serious concerns, the Mountain Lion Foundation suggests motion-activated devices that squirt blasts of cold water, play recordings of baying hounds or set off strobe lights as possible wildlife deterrents. These devices are most effective if moved or changed from time to time to prevent habituation. An aversive conditioning study of Florida panthers indicated it was possible to instill some degree of avoidance and fear of humans in cougars if such tactics were initiated early enough.

In the mid-2000s, the Washington Department of Fish and Wildlife (WDFW) began using Karelian dogs in their aversive reconditioning program. Fearless and tenacious, the medium-sized dogs with distinctive black and white markings are often used to hunt large, potentially aggressive game such as bear, moose and wild boar. In more recent years, they've been employed to sniff

Gail Loveman took this photograph of her Maine Coon cat, Zeus, and a young mountain lion going nose to nose at the sliding glass door of her home office in 2011. Loveman, who lives on a large acreage outside Boulder, Colorado, said she hasn't seen any sign of the lion since but has an air horn ready in case it decides to pay another visit. *Photo by Gail Loveman*

out, chase and deter bears and sometimes cougars that come near human use areas.

The dogs are an important component of a "hard release." This is when a tranquillized bear or cougar wakes up from its drug-induced nap surrounded by the roar of barking dogs, yelling humans and firecrackers, and possibly experiencing the sharp nip of a few pellets. That's often enough to convince the animal to stay away from humans. As of June 2012, the WDFW had four Karelian dogs, which are each paired with an enforcement officer for life. The program is funded solely by donations.

One thing cougar experts, organizations and wildlife officials agree on is the need for more public education. Even though Vancouver Island is the cougar capital of the world, many people living there don't know the proper way to respond if a cougar is seen—or may even be unaware that the big cats are present in the region. One long-time resident said she'd rather watch a cougar than attempt to scare it away if she saw one nearby. An avid jogger relatively new to Vancouver Island admitted she thought the "Cougar seen here on this date" signs she occasionally saw on running trails were a joke. And some people are convinced that "a healthy, well-fed cougar wouldn't attack a child in the company of two adults," or that they won't eat humans because they're "too bony."

Some schools teach children what to do if they see a bear or cougar, while community colleges and recreation centres occasionally offer similar courses to the public. In Wyoming, the Game and Fish Department has offered free "Staying Safe in Bear, Lion and Wolf Country" seminars to the public, and in some states, real estate agents have presented cougar awareness brochures to people purchasing rural properties.

Reading brochures pays off, too. In July 2007 a woman was approached by a cougar while hiking alone on a popular trail in Kootenay National Park in the Rocky Mountains of southeastern BC. According to an article in the *Calgary Herald*, the cat came within two metres (six feet) and reared up. The woman yelled, threw rocks and swung her backpack at it until it retreated and she was able to return to her vehicle. A park wildlife-conflict specialist said the woman did everything right, which probably saved her life. How did she know what to do? Shortly before arriving at the park she'd stopped at a visitor centre and read a brochure about how to respond to aggressive cougars.

The Washington Department of Fish and Wildlife uses Karelian dogs as part of a "hard release" when relocating problem bears and cougars. Yelling, fire crackers and a barking dog are often enough to persuade the predators to avoid humans. *Photo courtesy Washington Dept. of Fish and Wildlife Karelian Bear Dog Program*

Knowing what to do can prevent an encounter from turning into an attack, and may mean the difference between life and death if there is an attack. The afternoon of May 16, 2007, BC Ministry of Forests technician Wolfgang Beck was working in a proposed logging cut-block north of Sicamous when he glimpsed something moving out of the corner of his eye. He turned and saw a cougar running toward him. When he waved his arms and yelled the cougar stopped about five metres (sixteen feet) away. Still yelling and keeping his eyes locked on the cat's, Beck, who happened to have a hatchet in his right hand, grabbed his bear spray canister with his left hand. He squirted some of the spray to test the wind direction. The cougar was just out of reach of the mist and didn't react.

Beck kept yelling and waving an arm and after a couple of minutes the cougar moved off into thick brush. The fifty-one-year-old threw a few rocks after it and slowly left the cut-block, picking the most open route back to his truck. He remained on high alert and twice spotted the cougar following him. At the truck, Beck contacted his co-worker, who was working nearby, and they both vacated the area. What Beck found most unnerving was that during the standoff the cougar didn't make a sound, just stared straight at him with its ears forward. And when it vanished into the bush there was no noise at all.

Beck did everything right: he remained calm, acted aggressively at the first sight of the cougar and immediately prepared his defence. Even after the cat disappeared he remained alert and was wise enough to get himself and his colleague out of the vicinity. "I'm always very aware in the bush," said Beck, who camps, hikes and fishes and has worked in the bush for years. "I'd seen cougars before but only while driving. And I have noticed cougar tracks over the top of mine when hiking out at the end of the day. I knew the basics about what to do, but the bear and cougar safety course I took from Eyer Training Services just a few weeks before the encounter really helped. I don't know if I would have been able to handle the situation as well without that."

Studies confirm the need for more public education about cougars. In 2003, Winston Vickers of the UC Davis Wildlife Health Center conducted a survey of southern California residents regarding their feelings about mountain lions. Included were people living within the San Diego city boundary, as well as those adjacent to Cuyamaca Rancho State Park where numerous altercations and one human fatality had occurred in the 1990s. But twenty-three percent of rural residents and sixty-six percent of urban residents were unaware of their close proximity to lion habitat, which ranged from 1.5 to 40 kilometres (1 to 25 miles) respectively.

A 2008 research project for the Washington Department of Fish and Wildlife revealed that seventy-three percent of the people contacted did not know the most common reason for a cougar to attack (predatory instinct triggered by moving prey) and sixty-six percent did not know what to do if attacked (fight back). And more than fifty percent overestimated cougar-related injuries in the lower forty-eight states. Ninety-nine percent of the 1,200 residents surveyed felt mountain lions were an important and essential component of the ecosystem and have an inherent right to live in the state. And most believed people should accept responsibility for preventing conflicts with cougars. In the California survey, a large majority of urban and rural residents expressed positive feelings toward lions and a high tolerance for their presence. Many perceived their personal risk as low and indicated a willingness to modify their behaviour to coexist with lions. In comparison with similar studies in other states, California and Colorado residents appeared to be more positive about and accepting of lions than other states. Vickers speculated this may be associated with higher levels of education, income and urbanization, as well as consistent messages from wildlife officials and the media about the rarity of lion attacks and what to do if one occurs.

"A significant number of people value lions as part of the landscape and that matters a lot," noted Walter Boyce, wildlife veterinarian and professor at UC Davis. "The most important thing that can be done is to give people objective information so they can make their own decisions. The information shouldn't be biased for or against lions but should be the best scientific information about what lions do and how they live so people can make good decisions."

A 2001 to 2009 experiment in Washington attempted to do just that. Project CAT (Cougars and Teaching) was a collaboration between Washington Department of Fish and Wildlife, the Cle Elum/Roslyn School District and community members, as well as the University of Washington and Central Washington University. The unique program provided students and community members the opportunity to participate in hands-on field-work with cougar researchers. They gathered information, wrote reports, made casts of paw prints, collected and analysed scat, and observed cougars being radio collared.

According to researcher Gary Koehler, the children participating in the project had the most effect on changing attitudes about cougar ecology and helping people understand the role of cougars in their neighbourhood. Similar education programs involving young people have been conducted in other communities such as Jackson Hole, Wyoming, and Santa Monica, California.

The media exerts a powerful influence when it comes to public perceptions. In the past they've been criticized for sensationalizing attacks and accused of fostering the idea that there's a blood-thirsty cougar behind every bush. But aside from headlines such as

"Toddler snatched from killer jaws," recent newspaper accounts tend to include the facts of encounters as well as government guidelines on what to do if a person finds themselves in a similar situation.

Unfortunately, even those who should know the right answers sometimes get it wrong. In 2012, after a cougar was seen in a BC park, an employee told a television crew, "Cougars only attack if they're hurt or startled." That same year, an online US state trail guide warned people to "never make eye contact with a cougar." And a 2013 issue of a magazine published specifically for members of western Canada's fish and wildlife associations ran a story on cougars advising, "To protect oneself from becoming the target of aggression, eye contact should be avoided." Such inaccurate statements could have serious consequences. And even officials who provide correct information sometimes limit it to "make yourself look big, slowly back away and don't run," failing to mention the importance of loud, continuous noise, eye contact and aggressive behaviour to deterring a cougar.

Education, public awareness and involvement are important components of carnivore management and conservation. People need to take personal responsibility for their safety as well as liaise with government agencies to ensure sound strategies are applied. Anywhere there are people and cougars there will be some element of risk. It's up to humans to make that risk as small as possible.

In the early years of the last century, wolves and grizzly bears were, or nearly were, eradicated from large regions of Canada and the US. But somehow, despite the odds, cougars survived. Howard Quigley, who has been studying cougars for more than twenty-five years, once referred to them as "a supreme survivor, the most successful large predator in the western hemisphere." He attributes this accomplishment to their ability to adapt. The question is, are humans willing to adapt to cougars?

"I'd say the one big challenge across all cougar range is to get more information out to the public," Quigley said. "Agencies need to be more proactive about informing people how to live with this amazing animal. The fear factor scares me. There needs to be a certain level of understanding so people know how to live and behave in cougar country. That's the key to the future. Understanding the beauty of the animals and how to live with them, and not be afraid and want to destroy them."

Coexisting with cougars isn't about fear, it's about knowledge. To be successful it requires some modification of human behaviour and a tolerance for all wildlife, carnivores as well as the cute and cuddly. It means being aware and accountable, and recognizing the intricate balance of nature and the value of all creatures within it.

CHAPTER 14:
Wild & Beautiful

The mountain lion works a strong magic in the
imagination of many...It is the ultimate loner, a renegade
presence in the wildest canyons and wildest mountains,
the sign of everything that is remote from us,
everything we have not spoiled.

—DONALD SCHUELER, *Incident at Eagle Ranch*

The bed jiggled and a cold nose nudged my hand. Bailey needed a bathroom break. Our thirty-six-kilogram (eighty-pound) golden retriever–shepherd mix rarely goes out in the middle of the night. But he wanted out right then and, since Rick was away, I had to get up. The fir boards of the floor felt cool beneath my bare feet as I shuffled through the dark kitchen. I opened the door and was reaching for the screen when I heard the scream. *A woman's being murdered in the green space behind my yard!* I thought in horror.

I yanked Bailey back, slammed the door and leaned against it as if holding all the demons of hell at bay. *Call 911!* was my second thought. I heard the scream again and bolted for the bed, leapt in and pulled the covers over my head. I knew then that it was some kind of animal out there, not a woman. But the only being that came to mind was *Tsonqua*, the Wild Woman of the Woods in west coast First Nations lore. Lowering the covers slightly I peered at the French doors leading onto the deck and considered moving to an upstairs bedroom.

The next morning I googled animal screams and listened to coyotes, rabbits, owls and other creatures make unpleasant sounds until I found what I was looking for. A cougar had visited the green space the previous night. Although the big cats are extremely quiet, they do hiss, purr, growl and make bird-like chirps. And sometimes they scream. Lyn Hancock, author of *Love Affair with a Cougar*, has heard captive cougars scream when they were sick, desperate or females in heat. Judging by the internet sound bites, it was the latter I'd heard. I saw that the noise has been described as "a nerve-wracking, demoniac and terror-striking caterwaul." That summed it up well.

I heard the cougar scream years before I began this book. But it's something a person never forgets. I didn't know that experience would eventually take me on a journey that would include mock encounters with cougars in the backcountry of BC, as well as years of research and then more of writing.

I made one mistake while researching this book and it was a big one. I read every cougar attack description I could find over the course of two days. For the next week I flinched whenever Bailey entered the room and disturbing dreams interrupted my sleep. I wondered if I'd ever be able to walk in the woods again. Then one day I did. Yes, I was very aware of my surroundings. And yes, a cougar could have been lurking in the thick undergrowth along the side of the trails. I knew they passed through the neighbourhood searching for prey—and apparently boyfriends too. But not long into the walk I realized I didn't feel frightened, I felt confident. Because I knew what to do if I ran into one of the big cats.

People are fascinated by cougars. They're wild and beautiful, shy and secretive, curious and mysterious. They are compelling

Cougars are extremely quiet but they do growl, purr and hiss, as well as make bird-like chirps and occasionally shriek like a banshee.

icons of everything humans fear and admire. And sometimes they're deadly. Seeing a cougar is rare and being attacked by one even more so. But, as civilization continues to encroach on cougar habitat, the number of people living in and exploring rural and wilderness areas increases, and if cougar populations and territories continue to expand more interactions are inevitable. There will always be some level of risk. However, it can be reduced.

When asked if he thought humans and mountain lions could coexist, Winston Vickers of the UC Davis Wildlife Health Center replied, "It's clear that we do. The data shows that, in some places, we're coexisting at relatively close quarters without conflict. That happens fairly regularly around urban and exurban development. Given the low number of attacks and proximity of humans and lions, people aren't aware of just how much coexisting is going on."

We live on a small acreage on the outskirts of Courtenay on central Vancouver Island. One evening late in the summer of 2012, I was getting laundry off the clothesline, located thirty-three metres (thirty-six yards) from the house. Suddenly Bailey's hackles stood straight up and he crouched low to the ground, a steady growl rumbling from deep within his chest. The wild part of our property was about fourteen metres (fifteen yards) from where I stood. I scanned the tangle of trees, bushes and undergrowth but couldn't see anything.

A variety of wildlife crosses through the back of our property, and sometimes the occasional person. Whether it's a feral cat, deer, bear, bunny or someone who's strayed off the trail below, Bailey always runs to the post-and-wire fence and barks until we tell him it's okay. He'd done that for ten years. But now he was very slowly backing up toward the house. I hesitated for a few seconds then balanced the laundry basket between an arm and a hip, waved the other arm in the air and spoke firmly and loudly as I joined Bailey in a slow retreat to the back door.

Was it a cougar? Who knows? The following day when I met the next-door neighbour on the street, he asked if I'd seen any sign of bears lately. When I said no and asked why, he said he'd gone outside the night before and gotten a creepy feeling he'd never experienced in his more than two decades of living here. Just as I'd followed Bailey's cue, he'd paid heed to his intuition and gone back inside. Since that incident Rick has cleared the brush on the wild side of the fence to provide a better sightline from the house and yard and to make it less likely something big could sneak up on us.

Like most cats, cougars are curious and drawn to moving objects. Evidence indicates they watch and observe humans more frequently than most people realize. *Photo by Brad Boner, courtesy Panthera*

Working on this book generated a wide range of emotions. I was appalled to discover how humans had heedlessly killed cougars in the past and horrified by accounts of cougars attacking humans. Research on the cat's behaviour piqued my curiosity and I cried when I read about Max, the cougar confined to a barn stall for ten years. But most of all I felt awe at the power and grace of the cougar: the sleek and supple perfection of its body gliding through the landscape and leaping from precipices in absolute silence. At times the symmetrical beauty of the cat's facial markings moved me in an inexplicable way. And always I admired the carnivore's intense focus.

Over the centuries cougars have been revered, feared, persecuted and protected. As the dynamics of cougar–human relationships continue to evolve, I wonder about the future. How will people perceive cougars ten or one hundred years from now? And what impact will that have on cougars, people and the environment? In the meantime, I imagine cougars moving through shadowy forests and resting on sun-warmed rocks, living their mysterious lives mostly beyond human view. But watching us. And surviving.

APPENDIX:
Cougar Safety Checklist

- Be aware of your surroundings and cougar activity in the area.

- Supervise young children when they're outside; teach children what to do if they see a cougar or are attacked.

- Carry bear spray, a fixed-blade knife and a whistle or air horn.

- Never run from a cougar.

- Never turn your back on a cougar.

- While in cougar habitat, enjoy the outdoors with others when possible and stick together as a group.

- If you see a cougar, maintain direct eye contact and remove sunglasses.

- If the cougar is on a kill or with cubs put your hands in the air and speak firmly and loudly as you slowly back away, maintaining constant eye contact.

- If a cougar is seen, pick up small children and have short or vulnerable people stand behind others.

- If a cougar is seen and disappears, watch for it to circle around and follow.

- When leaving an area where a cougar has been seen, stick to open ground as much as possible. Do not run.

- If a cougar is watching, following or approaching, immediately act aggressively by throwing rocks, yelling, baring your teeth and growling. Make yourself appear larger by raising your arms above your head and holding your coat open or waving it overhead. Step up onto a rock or log if you can safely do so. Make loud, continuous noise by yelling or using a whistle or air horn.

- If a cougar charges, stand your ground, make noise and use whatever weapons you have.

- If attacked, fight back as hard as you can. Focus blows on the cougar's eyes and face and never give up.

- Never leave an attack victim alone.

- Leash dogs when hiking, and pay attention to their actions. Be aware that they may attract predators.

- Keep pets and livestock in secure enclosures at night.

- Don't feed deer or other wildlife that may attract predators.

- Clear underbrush 15 meters (50 feet) away from house and outbuildings. Install motion sensor lights around perimeter of house.

- Be extra cautious and alert when outside with your dog after dark.

SELECTED SOURCES

Interviews, Conversations and Other Personal Communications

WILDLIFE EXPERTS

Mike Badry, wildlife conflict manager, BC Ministry of Environment

Robyn Barfoot, curator, Cougar Mountain Zoo

Carole Baskin, founder and CEO, Big Cat Rescue

Mark Boyce, professor and Conservation Association Chair in Fisheries and Wildlife, University of Alberta

Walter Boyce, wildlife veterinarian and professor, University of California, Davis

Penny Dewar, cougar researcher

Jonah Evans, wildlife diversity biologist for the Trans Pecos Region, Texas Parks and Wildlife Department

Dave Eyer, wildlife expert and owner/operator of Eyer Training Services

Maurice Hornocker, founder, Hornocker Wildlife Institute and Selway Institute, and co-editor of *Cougar: Ecology and Conservation*

Marc Kenyon, black bear, mountain lion and wild pig programs coordinator, California Department of Fish and Wildlife

Rob Laidlaw, executive director, Zoocheck, and author of *Saving Lives and Changing Hearts: Animal Sanctuaries and Rescue Centers* and *Wild Animals in Captivity*

Jerry MacDermott, wildlife technician, BC Ministry of Forests, Lands and Natural Resource Operations

George Pedneault, cougar guide and tracker

Howard Quigley, director of the Teton Cougar Project and executive director of jaguar programs at Panthera

Harley Shaw, research biologist, Arizona Game and Fish Department (retired)

Lynda Sugasa, executive director, Safe Haven Rescue Zoo

Danielle Thompson, resource management and public safety specialist, Pacific Rim National Park Reserve

Winston Vickers, associate veterinarian, University of California, Davis, Wildlife Health Center

Ken Warren, public affairs officer, U.S. Fish and Wildlife Service–South Florida Ecological Services Office

Logan Wenham, senior public affairs officer, BC Ministry Forests, Lands and Natural Resource Operations

PERSONAL ACCOUNTS OF EXPERIENCES WITH COUGARS

Wolfgang Beck	Frank Hovenden
Stan Brock	Rick James
Liz Buckham	Harold Macey
Ruth Dickson	Summer McGee
Bob Evans	Suzanne Olszowiec
Clarence Hall	David Parker
Jim and Nell Hamm	Jack Scott
Lyn Hancock	Niki Wilson

ADDITIONAL SOURCES

Kristeva Dowling

Andy Everson

Brother Daniel Peterson, S.J.

Tom Phillips

Books

Baron, David. *The Beast in the Garden: A Modern Parable of Man and Nature.* New York: W.W. Norton & Company, 2004.

Brock, Stanley E. *More About LEEMO: The Adventures of a Puma.* New York: Taplinger Publishing Company, 1968.

Bruce, Jay C. *Cougar Killer.* New York: Comet Press Books, 1953.

Cougar Management Guidelines Working Group. *Cougar Management Guidelines.* Bainbridge Island, Washington: Wildfutures, 2005.

Deurbrouck, Jo, and Dean Miller. *Cat Attacks: True Stories and Hard Lessons from Cougar Country.* Seattle: Sasquatch Books, 2001.

Dickson, Ruth. *Pebbles in the Stream: River Rocks.* Comox, BC: GSG Ltd., 2010.

Dobbie, J. Frank. *The Ben Lilly Legend.* Texas: University of Texas Press, 1997.

Duncan, Eric. *Fifty-seven Years in the Comox Valley.* Courtenay, BC: The Comox Argus Co., 1934.

Etling, Kathy. *Cougar Attacks: Encounters of the Worst Kind.* Guilford, Connecticut: The Lyons Press, 2001.

Ewing, Susan, and Elizabeth Grossman. *Shadow Cat: Encountering the American Mountain Lion.* Seattle: Sasquatch Books, 1999.

Grey, Zane. *Roping Lions in the Grand Canyon.* New York: Harper & Brothers, 1924.

Haig-Brown, Roderick. *Panther.* Madeira Park, BC: Harbour Publishing, 2007.

Hall, Dell. *Island Gold.* Victoria, BC: Cougar Press Ltd., 1990.

Hancock, Lyn. *Love Affair with a Cougar.* Toronto: Doubleday Canada Limited, 1978.

Hibben, Frank C. *Hunting American Lions.* New York: Thomas Y. Crowell Company, 1948.

Hornocker, Maurice, and Sharon Negri, eds. *Cougar: Ecology and Conservation.* Chicago: University of Chicago Press, 2010.

Horsfield, Margaret. *Cougar Annie's Garden.* Nanaimo, BC: Salal Books, 1999.

Purdy, Al. *Cougar Hunter: A Memoir of Roderick Haig-Brown.* Vancouver: Phoenix Press, 1992.

Roosevelt, Theodore. *A Book-Lover's Holiday in the Open.* New York: Charles Scribner's Sons, 1916.

Saunders, Nicholas J., ed. *Icons of Power: Feline Symbolism in the Americas.* London & New York: Routledge, 1998.

Seton, Ernest Thompson. *Wild Animals at Home.* New York: Doubleday, Page and Co., 1923.

Shaw, Harley. *Soul Among Lions: The Cougar as Peaceful Adversary.* Arizona: University of Arizona Press, 2001.

Shelton, Gary. *Bear Encounter Survival Guide.* Hagensborg, BC: Pallister, 1997.

Courses

Bear & Cougar Rural and Recreational Course. Eyer Training Services, Clinton, BC.

Videos

American Cougar, National Geographic, 2011.

Online Resources

Big Cat Rescue: www.bigcatrescue.org.

Collins, Ken. "Bergie Solberg: Cougar Lady of the Sunshine Coast." www.geocities.ws/kensjournal/Bergie. Accessed June 2011.

Cougar Info: www.cougarinfo.org. A list of cougar attacks from 1890 to present begun by Paul Beier and continued by Linda Lewis.

The Cougar Network: www.cougarnet.org.

EKOS Communications, Inc. and Pacific Rim National Park Reserve. *Learning to Live with Large Carnivores: WildCoast Project Primer & Guidelines,* 2010. www.clayoquotbiosphere .org/wildcoast/docs/Wildcoast_Primer_v3.pdf.

Florida Panther Net: www.floridapanthernet.org.

Knopff, Kyle, Aliah Knopff and Michelle Bacon. "North of 49: Ongoing Cougar Research in Alberta, Canada" (www.cougarnet.org/Assests/SO9north.pdf). Accessed September 2011.

The Mountain Lion Foundation: www.mountainlion.org.

Ontario Puma Foundation: www.ontariopuma.ca.

Panthera, Leaders in Wild Cat Conservation: www.panthera.org.

Safe Haven Rescue Zoo: www.safehavenwildlife.com.

The Wild Felid Research and Management Association: www.wildfelid.com.

Zoocheck: www.zoocheck.com.

Articles, Reports and Related Materials

Bauer, Jim W., Kenneth A. Logan, Linda L. Sweanor and Walter M. Boyce. "Scavenging Behavior in Puma." *The Southwestern Naturalist* 50(4): 466–71, December 2005.

Eyer, Dave. *Bear & Cougar Encounters Course Handbook.*

Fitzhugh, E. Lee, Sabine Schmid-Holmes, Marc W. Kenyon and Kathy Etling. "Lessening the Impact of a Puma Attack on a Human." Proceedings of the 7th Mountain Lion Workshop at Ladner, Wyoming, 2003.

Hancock, Lyn. "A History of Changing Attitudes to *Felis concolor.*" Master's thesis, Simon Fraser University, 1980.

Knopff, K., and M.S. Boyce. "Prey Specialization by Individual Cougars (*Puma concolor*) in Multi-prey Systems." Transactions of the North American Wildlife and Natural Resources Conference 72: 194–210, 2007.

Mattson, David, Kenneth Logan and Linda Sweanor. "Factors Governing Risk of Cougar Attacks on Humans." *Human–Wildlife Interactions* 5(1): 135–58, Spring 2011.

Schnarr family fonds. Campbell River Museum.

Smith, Swain Elinor. *The Nine Lives of Cougar Smith.* Unpublished manuscript.

Sweanor, Linda L., Kenneth A. Logan, Jim W. Bauer, Blue Millsap and Walter M. Boyce. "Puma and Human Spatial and Temporal Use of a Popular California State Park." *Wildlife Management* 72(5): 1076–84, 2008.

Thompson, Danielle M. "Noninvasive Approaches to Reduce Human-cougar Conflict in Protected Areas of the West Coast of Vancouver Island." Master's thesis, University of Victoria, 2010.

Vickers, W. "Attitudes Toward and Acceptance of Mountain Lions by Urban and Rural Southern Californians and Comparison of other Western States." Unpublished paper.

Statistics

Unless otherwise specified, statistics in this book were compiled from data obtained from the British Columbia Ministry of Environment, the Cougar Info website (www.cougarinfo.org), *Cougar Attacks: Encounters of the Worst Kind* by Kathy Etling, the California Department of Fish and Wildlife website, *Two Admirals: Sir Fairfax Moresby & John Moresby, a Record of a Hundred Years* by John Moresby, a 2012 article by Dan MacLennan in the *Campbell River Courier-Islander* titled "75-year-old woman fends off cougars in harrowing attack on her little dog" and directly from attack victims. The data is based on documented attacks and fatalities from the early 1800s through the end of 2012.

ACKNOWLEDGEMENTS

This book wouldn't have been possible without Dave Eyer of Eyer Training Services. Before we even met in person, he offered to help in any way possible. Little did he realize that would involve reading the entire manuscript twice and answering endless questions about cougar scat, eyeshine, the difference between pistols and revolvers, what to do if a person encountered three cougars at once and so much more. Dave devoted countless hours to developing a database of all cougar attacks on humans from the early 1800s to 2012 and then provided a dazzling array of charts, graphs and statistical analysis based on it. Without fail, he was always there to offer assistance and encouragement.

Many people contributed to my understanding and knowledge of cougars. I send a heartfelt thank you to the many biologists, government employees and scientists who so generously shared their expertise and data. And to Robyn Barfoot of Cougar Mountain Zoo, Stan Brock and Lyn Hancock, who provided insights into the lives of captive cougars. I would also like to acknowledge Carole Baskin of Big Cat Rescue and Rob Laidlaw of Zoocheck for their information on captive wildlife laws and the appalling living conditions of some cougars.

A big part of this book concerns cougar awareness, safety and defence. I'm extremely grateful to all who shared their personal encounters. Their courage and resourcefulness is truly inspiring. And it would not have been possible to incorporate their stories into the larger picture of human-cougar interactions without the comprehensive records that have been compiled by Paul Beier, Linda Lewis and others.

A huge thanks as well to those who donated photographs, and to the professional team at Douglas & McIntyre and Harbour Publishing for all their behind-the-scenes efforts in design, production, marketing, sales and everything else that goes into a book. And to Pam Robertson, my editor. She prodded me to dig deeper and the book is better for it.

And, as always, a special thank you to my partner, Rick, for his support on so many levels during all my creative projects.

INDEX

Page numbers in **bold** refer to illustrations, tables and charts.